RED BEANS & TATERS

A TRUE STORY ABOUT GROWING UP POOR IN SMALL TOWN TEXAS

JOHN CONN

outskirts
press

Red Beans & Taters
A true story about growing up poor in small town Texas
All Rights Reserved.
Copyright © 2017 John Conn
v2.0

The opinions expressed in this manuscript are solely the opinions of the author and do not represent the opinions or thoughts of the publisher. The author has represented and warranted full ownership and/or legal right to publish all the materials in this book.

This book may not be reproduced, transmitted, or stored in whole or in part by any means, including graphic, electronic, or mechanical without the express written consent of the publisher except in the case of brief quotations embodied in critical articles and reviews.

Outskirts Press, Inc.
http://www.outskirtspress.com

ISBN: 978-1-4787-7188-3

Cover Photo © 2017 thinkstockphotos.com. All rights reserved - used with permission.

Outskirts Press and the "OP" logo are trademarks belonging to Outskirts Press, Inc.

PRINTED IN THE UNITED STATES OF AMERICA

Table of Contents

1. So It Begins 1
2. The Family 5
3. The Biological Dad 17
4. The Real Dad 20
5. On The Move, Again 26
6. The Summer Of 1971 35
7. Back to the Story 48
8. Fall Of '71 52
9. The Summer Of '72 61
10. The Fall Of '72 73
11. Spring Of '73 85
12. Fall Of '73 88
13. The Winter Of '74 94
14. The Summer Of '75 100
15. Winter Of '75 103
16. November '75 104

CHAPTER 1

So It Begins

"THEY'RE HOME! THEY'RE HOME!" someone was yelling from the front of the house; then it sounded like a small herd of cattle running to the front door. The screen door was slamming open and shut like we were all being shot out of a cannon.

It was Wednesday August 11, 1971, a typical scorching hot Texas day. It was probably 105 degrees in the shade. A couple of my brothers and I were playing on the back porch; we took off, running like crazy when we heard the call to arms. The other kids were already in the house probably watching television.

Daddy had left early that morning to go get Momma from the hospital. I remember it being weird because he wasn't at work. It was one of only maybe two days I ever remember him missing work. Momma wasn't sick or anything; she was just having a baby. Daddy had gone to get her and Linda Michelle Harris; we just called her Shelly, the tenth child in our family. You would think that after the eighth or ninth, the excitement might not be as great for the tenth, but it was still exciting. So here she came.

Shelly was a redhead with plenty of freckles. In fact, she was the only redheaded child of the bunch. I don't know of anyone on either side of my mom's or dad's family having red hair either, but Shelly sure did. Me, I am one of the four dirty blonds in the family and kind of stuck in the middle. There are four boys older than me, one boy younger, and now four girls younger.

Rocky is the oldest followed by Andrew (Andy), then Jerry, then Robert, then me. After me, God decided Momma needed some girls: Dawn (Sissy), then Sherrill, then another boy, James (Jaimie), then Patricia, and finally Shelly. Momma was seventeen when she had Rocky and thirty-two when she had Shelly. Think about that, ten kids in fifteen years, all single births, no twins.

I was eight when Shelly was born and I remember the day she came home perfectly well. There is nothing I can think of that makes me remember it as well as I do; it is not like there was a major world event or turning point in my life or anything like that. After all she was the tenth child of the family. I just know that I have a very vivid memory of that day.

They turned in the dirt driveway in my dad's '57 Chevy, which is kind of a hot rod for a man who was bringing home his wife and a baby, the tenth child. Momma was sitting in the front seat holding Shelly in her lap. Car seats were not an issue back then; in fact, I don't think we even had one. Of course Daddy was driving. As they came rolling up to the

SO IT BEGINS

house we were all trying to look in Momma's window to see, but since I was kind of the runt of the litter, my point of view was basically belly buttons and a door handle. The youngest were screaming for someone to hold them up, but no one was listening. With the car stopped and everyone crowding around, my dad comes walking around the front of the car yelling, "Move back away from the front of the car, damn it! All of you move back." Then Momma stepped out holding the new baby.

Before we move ahead, let me give you a little history on the family. Marilyn Ruth Gann, Momma, was born on December 19, 1939 in a cedar patch near Breckenridge, Texas, which is a small farming town between Abilene and Fort Worth. Momma was your typical farm girl. Somewhat husky or big-boned as was the description Granny always used. I think having ten children may tend to add a little to your structure over the years. Probably just carrying around a baby all of those years would do it, forgetting all of the other work that goes into being a mother of ten.

Momma was about five foot, nine inches tall and may have weighed about 150 pounds. She was beautiful with long brown hair. I don't really remember her ever wearing very much makeup or anything like that, but I remember her striking facial features. She had big brown eyes and very strong cheekbones.

I am sure the loving, caring, nurturing instincts of a mother can be sucked out of a woman real quick when dealing with ten kids, so it may have been that we kids didn't see what others saw in Momma. We saw the mean looks, the harsh words, the spankings, and the word of the law, but as far back as I can remember, nobody ever called her Marilyn. Everyone called her either Sister or her most common name, "Love." I can't imagine how she stretched herself in as many directions as I am sure she had to in order to satisfy the wants and needs of that many children at so many different ages. The little ones needed hugging, changing, feeding, and lots of a mother's attention. The middle ones need hugging, playing, questions answered, more questions answered, doctoring, and a smack on the bottom. The older ones needed a lot more smacks, guidance, direction, and lots of "no's." Momma was truly remarkable in her abilities to do all of these things. On the other hand one has to ask, "What in the hell is this woman thinking? Why would anyone have ten kids on purpose?"

CHAPTER 2

The Family

A LOOK BACK at the parents' family might explain this question. I think Momma was a product of her own family and environment. Families in the forties and fifties were farm families, needing large families to work the farm. While Momma's family didn't own a farm, they lived on one in the country. She was the fifth of eight children born to Henry and Maimi Gann. The oldest was Henry, named after Grandpa; next was Melvin, then Francis, Dale, Momma, then Linda, Jackie, and finally Ricky. I never knew my grandpa Henry, but I saw pictures of him. I think he died when Momma and her siblings were very young. The only grandpa I knew was Carlos Trejo, my granny's second husband; everyone just called him Shorty. They were Pawpaw and Granny to us. Pawpaw had five kids of his own so together they had thirteen. None of the thirteen kids graduated from high school. My momma finished the tenth grade.

Granny was old school and hard to the core. She loved to tell the story of my momma being born in the cedar patch. This was her medal of war, badge of courage, or maybe just her way of bragging. She could never understand why women these days had to take off from work just to have a baby. She cut down seventy-five cedar posts with a two-headed axe the day she had Momma. In fact, she was in the field when she went into labor. The black lady who lived down the road delivered the baby right there on the spot. Granny's famous quote, as politically incorrect as it is, was, "Your momma was named Marilyn after the old nigger woman that delivered her that day." Granny said that Marilyn told her she was gonna have a girl and she better name her Marilyn 'cause they was best friends. Even twenty years later, Granny still teared up when she talked about her neighbor and best friend Marilyn. Together they raised nineteen kids in that cedar patch, they spanked each other's kids when they needed it, and they shared food when the other needed it, but above all, she was Granny's best friend and I think they shared strength when the other needed it. Naming my mom after Marilyn was Granny's show of love and appreciation. She used to say that Marilyn could and would stand up to anyone and was stronger than most men.

All but one of my mom's siblings were born at home. The youngest of the eight, Ricky, was the only one born in a hospital. Granny was a big woman. I think she may have weighed in at just a biscuit over 250 pounds and I swear I never saw her with more than three or four teeth in her mouth. If you were to look up "good old farm girl" in the dictionary it would have a picture of Granny Gann. At any given time around her house you would find at least a hundred chickens, several ducks, at least five dogs, maybe a goat or two, and sometimes a pig. Granny always had a small garden with your basic vegetables like tomatoes, okra, and whatever else she could get to grow. She ate what she wanted, lived the way she wanted to live, and was happy about it.

Her big love and reason for living was wrestling. Not the theatrical, show time, made for television crap that you see today with the WWF and all that, but the original good old days of the good guys beating the bad guys. Every Saturday night you could either watch it on television (local channel 11) or you could go see it live in Dallas. *Saturday Night Wrestling* was filmed in Dallas at the Sportatorium. There would be four or five matches with an occasional women's match and sometimes even a match between midgets. The local heroes were the Von Erich family. Fritz Von Erich was the main man. He was the creator of the "Claw," a fierce and brutal move that he used to subdue the bad guy. Basically he would use his right hand to squeeze the forehead, with his thumb on one temple and his fingers spread out over the top of your head, and squeeze until he split your head open or until you gave up. It was a great move in the seventies. Granny had more pictures of the Von Erich family in her house than pictures of her kids or grandkids.

She could be found at the Sportatorium every Saturday night. Before the fights began, she would set up shop outside and sell eggs to all the regular spectators and the locals. Pawpaw worked at the event, parking cars. Everyone knew Shorty and Maimie. Granny would spend the evening inside cheering for the good guys and booing the bad guys. You can't really argue with the way they lived, because they both lived well into their eighties. Maybe bacon, chitlins, and fried everything are the secret to long life. Anyway, they were the cornerstones of the family.

RED BEANS & TATERS

Pawpaw worked hard all of his life. He was about five-foot-six and weighed about two hundred pounds. He always had somewhat of a limp. I think one leg was a little shorter than the other, hence his nickname "Shorty." He smoked two to three packs of cigarettes a day, drank a few beers every day, and was good as gold to Granny. He never complained about things and was always ready to do something funny to us kids. I don't know when he came to the United States but I do know he spoke Spanish a lot better than he spoke English. The only job I ever knew of him occupying was with the JC Duncan Waste Management Company. He used to ride on the back of the trash trucks and pick up trash. I remember when he got promoted to driver. That was a great day in his life, no more picking up the heavy trash. Now all he had to do was drive the truck. He worked hard at work and he worked hard at home. He always considered himself lucky to have such a good job. Not only did he get paid to do what he did, but he also had first choice of lots of great stuff that people would throw away. I would be willing to bet that 80 percent of everything in our house came from his job. He could never understand why people threw away such good stuff, ranging from clothes to dishes to furniture.

Henry was my mom's oldest brother. I don't remember Uncle Henry very much because he was in the Army all of his life and was never around. Momma had a few pictures of him in his Army greens. He was stationed in Germany for what seems like forever and when he came back to the States he was stationed in North Carolina. He would visit every now and then, but that was it.

The next one in line was Melvin. Uncle Melvin also spent a

THE FAMILY

few years in the Army but not very long. He lived either in Texas or in Missouri most of his life. Missouri is where his wife's family was from. He and Shirley got married when they were young. They had five children, all girls. Melvin always said the army removed the wrong testicle when he had surgery, so he couldn't have any boys. Melvin was the "always down on my luck" relative. He always had trouble holding a job and nothing ever seemed to go his way. I don't know why he had such bad luck. It is not like he drank very much, and he was somewhat of a nice guy but he just never seemed to get a break. Even in our little nickel/dime poker games that we played at our house, Melvin always seemed to be the big loser. Of course he didn't care most of the time because he wasn't losing his money. He always played with borrowed money. A dollar from one person, fifty cents from another, and he was in the game. The best thing about Melvin was his tattoos. He had five or six of them and they ranged from a small Jesus to an R-rated, full-bodied lady on the underside of his upper left arm. He also had a funny one (funny to boys ages ten to thirteen). It was a seventy-ish-year-old lady with a see-through negligee on his back. We used to marvel at Melvin's ability and willingness to drink a cup of steaming hot black coffee regardless of what time of day or night and regardless of the temperature outside. It could be thirty degrees or 130 degrees and Melvin would be drinking coffee. Shirley was always shy and reserved. She never really said much of anything unless Melvin was losing what little bit of money he had, playing poker.

Third sibling in Momma's family was Francis. She was just a year older than Momma. I don't have very many memories of Aunt Francis either, because she married a military man and lived in Germany most of her life. I do remember her coming home a couple of times to visit but that is about it.

Uncle Dale was next in line and he was probably my favorite uncle because he was funny and he usually brought us something good when he came to visit. He lived in Mineral Wells his entire life and from a financial standpoint, Dale was the most successful in my mom's family. He drove a truck for years and then bought his own truck and eventually had his own trucking company. I remember when he would come visit he always brought us something. To show the state of mind of our family, I am not talking about toys and stuff; he brought food or clothes and furniture. I remember the day he brought a dining room table that was huge and round. It had ten plastic stacking chairs. This was the best thing I had ever seen. Our family used that table and chairs for as long as I could remember, and then one of my brothers used it for years after we all had moved. Dale was married to Linda and I always thought they were the perfect couple. Dale was tall, dark-haired, and I guess good-looking for a rough and rugged truck-driving farm boy. They had three girls and no boys. There seems to be a pattern brewing. All of my cousins are girls.

My mom's three younger siblings also lived in our area their entire life. Aunt Linda married Charles Jackson when she was seventeen. Charles' family was like ours as well. He had four brothers and I think three sisters, none of whom graduated from high school. Aunt Linda was as rough and mean as any of the men I knew. She was built like Momma, kind of husky with dark hair. We thought Linda was cool because she also had tattoos. She had some on her arms and some on her

THE FAMILY

hands. Unlike my uncle Melvin though, I don't think Linda got any of hers while she was in prison. Linda was tough and had no problem proving it. She wrestled with us boys and played football just like a man.

My uncle Jackie was like Melvin in that if it weren't for bad luck, he wouldn't have had any luck at all. Jackie was married three times that I know of and had kids with all three wives. He spent several stints in jail for various things, but nothing really bad, mainly traffic violations. Jackie was somewhat the sensible one of the bunch, but always seemed to be out of work or out of a place to live. So he stayed with us on several occasions.

Ricky Don was the baby of the family. Uncle Ricky never got married. It seems as though he was the chosen one to stay at home and take care of Pawpaw and Granny. He lived with them until they both passed away. Ricky was about the same age as my oldest brother Rocky so he seemed more like a cousin to us than an uncle. I don't think Ricky went to school past the sixth grade. Unlike most of his brothers he was never in any kind of trouble with the law. He just worked hard at a number of menial jobs.

For the most part my aunts and uncles were country rednecks. While they never thought they were better than anyone else, they damn sure didn't think anyone was better than them. I think they were your typical southern farm family with very little education, very little ambition, and were accepting of the fact that being poor was their destiny. At one time or another four or five of my mom's siblings and their families lived with us for various amounts of time. As rough and mean as they were to the rest of the world, I think they really loved each other and would do anything for each other. However, they would rather be damned to hell forever than actually say it out loud.

I don't recall my mom being much different from her brothers and sisters except in what she wanted for her kids. I think she was more of the mothering type. For example, my mom never had a tattoo; in fact I don't think she even had her ears pierced. I remember she had clip-on earrings that she never wore. Momma was not the rough and tough type. Unlike my aunt Linda, whom I can recall a couple of times getting into a fight and I mean a fist-throwing type of fight, not a yelling and screaming, pull your hair kind of fight. Linda was meaner than most men I ever knew. Momma never said that she was ashamed of her upbringing or her siblings, but she always made it clear to us that she wanted and expected more out of her children. Now don't let this touchy, feely stuff about my mom give you any misconceptions about her lack of parenting skills or her willingness to kick ass when necessary. She was still a farm girl and keep in mind that we were growing up in the "It is okay to spank your children" era. Momma could be just as mean as the rest of them.

I remember right after Shelly was born, Aunt Linda and Uncle Charles were at our house with their two kids, Charles Joe and Donna. Donna was born just a few months before Shelly. This day stands out in my mind because it was the first and only time I recall my momma in a real fight. Momma was talking about a stroller that she saw for sale at a garage sale in Grand Prairie but she didn't have the money to buy it, so when Daddy got home later that day she was going back to

THE FAMILY

get it. A few hours later we pulled up to the house where the stroller was for sale and shut my mouth, there were Aunt Linda, Uncle Charles, and their two kids buying Momma's stroller. Keep in mind, Momma and Linda both had just recently given birth only a month or so ago. Momma jumped out of the car before my dad had even come to a complete stop; she ran over to Aunt Linda and grabbed her in a headlock and threw her down. I guess watching Saturday Night Wrestling teaches you how to handle a situation such as this. After a few minutes of on-the-ground wrestling, my aunt got up and grabbed the stroller and was heading to her car. Then came Momma, who grabbed the other end of the stroller, and the tug of war began. I would like to point out that both my uncle and my dad were leaning against the car talking by this time. Meanwhile, as children should, about four of us jumped on my aunt just long enough for Momma to get the stroller. I don't know who paid for it but I do know that Momma ended up with the stroller. One good thing about our family is that nothing bad lasts very long. The very next weekend, Aunt Linda and her family were at our house. I remember the grownups laughing about the fight and Aunt Linda making fun of Momma. She said Momma must be getting old because she needed her kids to help her beat up her little sister.

As with any situation where there are a lot of people in a small area, things happen, stuff gets broken or misplaced, things turn up missing, and so on. Well, our house was no different. The difference was in the actions taken afterward. I am sure Momma got it right most of the time, just by sheer motherly instincts, but I know for a fact there were times when the innocent were punished and the guilty were set free. We did not adhere to the "Telling the truth is always the best policy" theory when we were kids. If you could get away with something, that was usually the best way to go. We were not a "Go to your room and think about what you did" kind of family either. We were a "Spare the rod, spoil the child" kind of family. If Daddy was slapping you across the head for something you didn't do, it was always followed with a comment such as, "I'm sure you did something that I don't know about." Momma was more judicial in her approach. She would almost always ask, as if she felt that someday it would work, "Who did this?" After repeating the question several times, the next statement was always, "If I don't find out who did this, every one of you will get a whippin'!" As one of the youngest, I learned real quickly that if something happened or something was broken, someone would get a whippin'. Momma usually started with the oldest and by the time she got to me, she was usually tired, so the best scenario was to just keep quiet.

Momma was never one of those moms who said, "You just wait until your father gets home!" She took care of her own business. I remember a couple of times that one of my brothers got the bright idea of running outside and hiding, but Momma would always have a life lesson for that person. She would stand at the door and yell something like, "You're gonna get hungry sometime!" or "It will be dark in a few hours!" or "If you're gonna leave be sure and take all your stuff so you don't have to come back!" If you think about these three things, you realize that she was pointing out the three basics. 1) You always need food. 2) You always need a place to sleep, and 3) You can always come back home.

I don't claim to be the smartest in my family but I really

THE FAMILY

think I learned the quickest. For example, I remember one of my brothers hiding under the bed from my mom. Well, the first time this happened I recall my mom getting the long, wooden-handled broom. Let's just say that I knew from that moment on, hiding under a bed was not a good choice, but my brothers seemed to have forgotten and a couple of them used the "hiding under the bed" trick again, but ended up with the same result. Another thing I learned rather early was not to grab whatever it was Momma was whipping you with. This just made her mad. I also learned that if you kind of went around in circles while she had your arm and was whipping you, it didn't hurt as bad. Being somewhat educated now, I know it was because your body was moving in the same direction as the object striking your body rather than striking you in a stationary position; back then I just knew that it didn't hurt as much. I was sometimes referred to as a crybaby by my older brothers but again, it was a tactic I learned very early. If during a whipping I would start crying, the whipping would not last very long. I think my brothers thought it would stunt their manhood if they cried, so it seemed their whippings would last longer. Crying also helped if one of them was beating me up or just hurting me in general. The unwritten rule was "deal with it." But I figured out that if the situation got to a crying point, Mom would step in.

Another area I learned very quickly in was the car. Anytime we were in the car there was definitely going to be trouble. Imagine as many as six or eight kids in the backseat of a car. That is a lot of "don't touch me," "you're on my side," and "get off me!" When it came to the point where Momma was going to start smacking people I learned that if you were on the bottom of the pile, or on the floorboard, you had a lot less chance of getting hit. Please don't think that my mom and dad abused us, because that was not the case. We probably deserved a lot more whippings than we actually got. Again, we grew up in a time when it was normal to spank your child. Many parents, as did all of my aunts and uncles and probably most all parents during that time, lacked the "modern day" parenting skills. We couldn't be threatened with losing the television or computer for a week because we didn't have a computer and sometimes we didn't have a television. We couldn't be grounded from going to a friend's house or having friends over because we lived so far out in the country that friends coming over rarely happened anyway. We couldn't even be grounded from the telephone because we didn't have a phone until I was seventeen years old.

Children will do as their parents did. My mom and dad grew up in a time when things were tough, people were not as educated, and rearing a child was your own business. I remember comments from my uncles, as one of us would do something stupid or wrong. They would say to my mom or dad, "Can you imagine what a beating we would have gotten if we had done something like that?" Remembering comments like that makes me realize that my mom and dad really tried to be better parents than what their parents were. I think my mom tried real hard to make things better for us so we wouldn't be in the same situation as she was. She wasn't ashamed of our family but she always wanted us to do better.

CHAPTER 3

The Biological Dad

I DON'T KNOW how my mom met Herschel Conn, but I suspect it was while he was in the army. Mineral Wells is just a few miles from Breckenridge, and Herschel was stationed at Ft. Wolters several times so I think they must have met there. While Herschel is my biological father, I will never refer to him as my dad.

The story of Herschel is not clear even to this day but here is my best recollection of what happened. He and my mom got married when she was just sixteen or seventeen. Based on the age of my oldest brother, Rocky, I think they had to get married. Rocky was born in Mineral Wells when Momma was seventeen. Based on the birthplaces of all of us I guess that Herschel's military duties moved our family around quite a bit. Andy was born in Massachusetts, Jerry and Robert was both born in Germany, and I was born back here in Mineral Wells, Texas. Sissy was born in Anchorage, Alaska, and Sherrill was born at Parkland Hospital in Dallas, Texas.

The last family moment I recall with Herschel is what I believe to be the day he left us; I think I was four years old. Again, this is only my recollection; no one in my family ever discussed his departure with me. I guess I could have asked one of my brothers or my mom but I never did and they never offered. Remember, our family was never a sharing, caring type of family. Emotion was not in our family creed. Anyway, the only memory I have of Herschel leaving could just as well be a dream that I have convinced myself is the truth, but over the years I have heard similar stories that add credibility to my story. I remember three or four of us taking a bath and Herschel sticking his head in the bathroom and saying, "I am going to the store and the first one out gets to go with me." Robert was the first one out and God as my witness, that was the last time I remember seeing either of them until Herschel showed up at my elementary school one day and ate lunch with Andy, Jerry, and myself. Grandmother Conn was with him and I remember going over to her; after all, she was still my grandmother. I didn't even recognize Herschel sitting in the chair across the room. Robert was not with them. Herschel continued to come to eat lunch with us a couple of more times over the years after that, I think about three times, but that was the extent of his presence. There were never any birthday or Christmas presents, no letters, and since we never had a phone, there were no phone calls. The true story of why Robert was the only one to go live with Herschel and the other six of us stayed with my mom is another one of the "never discussed, never told" stories. That is just the way it was. There were a few pictures of Herschel in an old suitcase but nothing that the family sat and reminisced over. Herschel was simply someone who was there, but then was gone; there are vague memories but nothing major. My older brothers probably have better memories or at least more of

THE BIOLOGICAL DAD

them, but for Sissy, Sherrill, and me, we were all too young to remember. Sherrill was about a year old, Sissy was three, and I was four. Momma never said Herschel left us; this is just my version of what happened. Momma never spoke of him at all. There were rumors that one possible reason for his departure was that Sherrill was not his child. Remember, Herschel was in the military and was gone at times.

CHAPTER 4

The Real Dad

THE RUMOR IS that Sherrill is actually the first child born to Billie Harris (my soon-to-be stepdad) and Momma. While Sherrill holds the Conn name, I think she may actually show a strong resemblance to Billie, whom I will refer to as my dad from now on. With the exception of the few aforementioned memories of Herschel, I don't remember any other dad but Billie Harris. He is and always will be my dad.

Billie James Harris is your typical *drop out of junior high to work the farm and support the family* country boy just like Momma's family. He grew up in Lubbock, Texas, picking cotton and working the family farm twelve to fourteen hours a day. He is country to the core, with dark hair, a perpetual farmer's tan, and a hard, rough look. As a child, I never saw my dad wear anything but a pair of cowboy boots, jeans, and usually a button-down shirt. Sometimes he wore coveralls over his jeans and shirt but usually as a means of keeping warm. As an adult, I can say that I may have seen him wear a pair of tennis shoes a handful of times, but other than that, I have never seen him wear anything but cowboy

THE REAL DAD

boots. At my wedding, he wore a tuxedo with the understanding he was wearing boots. He loves to tell the stories of him and his brothers with their souped-up race cars and all the hell they raised in Lubbock. He may not have been intelligent in the sense of education, but he was by far one of the smartest men I ever knew. He was smart with common sense and logic. While he always had some saying to go with almost any situation, he was really a quiet man. I think his shyness came from a slight speech impediment. Daddy had what we called a harelip, which probably is not the correct term, but that's what we called it. He couldn't pronounce his S's, R's or L's very well. For instance when he said "snake," it would come out "nake." His L's came out more like a "W" sound. I remember one day he came home from work and he was yelling because dinner wasn't ready yet. He yelled out, "I am hungry; all I had to eat today was two lemons and an RC." Royal Crown cola was a brand of soda that was very popular in the sixties and seventies, especially with the country and black folk. It was the only soda I remember my dad drinking. Anyway, what he meant to say was one thing, but of course with his inability to pronounce an "L" properly, we all got a big laugh and especially my mom, because what we heard was, "I am hungwy, aw I had to eat today was two women and a RC." To this day that is one of our favorite lines.

Daddy was a hardworking man who will work hard until the day he dies. He smokes three packs of cigarettes a day, always has and always will, he drinks real beer (he used to drink Schlitz), and I bet he has only been to the doctor maybe three or four times in his life. His theory was you only go to the doctor when there is a bone sticking through the skin or the bleeding won't stop. I don't think he has ever missed a day of work because he was sick.

Daddy worked at a gas station in Grand Prairie for what seems like forever. I don't know when he started working there, but this is the first job I remember him having. He was somewhat of a small man physically, maybe five-foot-eight or nine, and he may have weighed 135 or 140 pounds soaking wet. He was hard on the exterior, with a rugged face and dark hair; his hands were the hands of someone who has worked hard all of his life. He was not the emotional type at all, but then again, neither was my mom or anyone else in our family. As a young boy if you hurt yourself and you needed less than an amputation, you had better not cry, because then the whole family got to make fun of you for being a wimp or crybaby.

My dad came from a large family as well. Counting stepbrothers and sisters, he had twelve siblings. The only brother or sister of his that I ever met was Larry. All of my dad's other brothers and sisters lived in either the panhandle of Texas or in New Mexico, but we never met them. Like Momma, Daddy grew up in the time when you had to have large families to help work the farm. He tells of the years he grew up in Lubbock, Texas, picking cotton and farming all his life. He quit school in the sixth grade to work the farm full time, as did most of his brothers and sisters. While not an educated man he always appeared to be smart. Although he never said it or really showed it I know my dad loved all of us as if we were his own.

His job at the gas station was to pump gas (back then all gas stations were full service) and be a mechanic. I always

THE REAL DAD

thought there was nothing my dad couldn't fix on a car. Cars were his passion. I mentioned earlier that I remember his '57 Chevy. That car was sweet. I remember listening to his Elvis eight-tracks and how that car would fly. I spent evenings at the station with him while he worked. He even let me pump some gas and check the air in some tires. We used to play on the racks that raised the cars up and down. I loved watching my dad work on the cars because he knew everything about them. The man who owned the station Daddy worked at was Wayne Marks. Wayne was very good to my dad and our family as I remember. I think he meant a lot to my dad as well because Daddy named his firstborn son James Wayne. James was my dad's middle name and Wayne from his boss.

At the time Shelly was born, my mom wasn't working and my dad now worked at a different gas station in Grand Prairie. I don't remember exactly what happened, but I think Mr. Marks died, and the station closed down.

My dad went to work for one of the new Exxon Car Care Centers. Again, our family was never the touchy feely, express your feelings, share with kids and that kind of stuff, but I remember my dad not being the same after he changed jobs. I think he missed Wayne. Shortly after that, Daddy started driving a truck for a company called Trans Tex Supply Company. This was a great deal for us because he was happy and he made more money. He would work there for the next ten or twelve years.

I think the fact that my dad was willing to marry a woman with seven kids is either a testament to his love for her or confirmation of his insanity. Since they went on to have three more children of their own, it was probably the former. Daddy was much like Momma in the emotional department. There was never a family time or anything like that. Tenderness, togetherness, sharing and caring were things we saw on *Leave It to Beaver*.

Daddy never said much, but when he spoke, we listened, most of the time. "Ain't no sense in complaining about something you don't have, 'cause it ain't going to git you nothin' anyway," was one of his most profound statements. There are several things Daddy used to say that, while I may not say them to my kids, I know helped shape me as an adult. He was a man who may not have been satisfied with the way his life turned out or the job he had and how much money he made, but he never complained, he was never jealous or envious of someone else, and he never made excuses about anything. I remember the first time I had a friend from school come over to spend the night. His name was Joe Holman. Joe and I were best friends and would be for the next fifteen years. Anyway, we were in the fourth grade and I had already spent the night at Joe's house a couple of times and it was great. They weren't rich by any means, but they ate meat every night for dinner. You have to understand that I was used to eating red beans and potatoes for dinner almost every day. Meat was something that we got maybe once a week when Daddy got paid, usually fried chicken. The other great thing about Joe's house was that everyone had their own bed. In fact the three boys shared a bedroom and his sister had her own room. Anyway I remember Joe sitting down to eat dinner at our house and looking around he asked, "Where's the meat?" Without ever raising his head up my dad just said, "Boy, this may not be meat but it will put meat on your bones, so eat!" No long

THE REAL DAD

speeches, no sermons, just a simple statement and it was done.

Daddy loved the simple things like fishing, working on cars, and occasionally playing with the kids. For an old man (what dad isn't an old man to his kids), he could still get around great. There were many times when he would play football or baseball with us. We went fishing every now and then but none of us liked it as much as Daddy. He could sit there for hours and never even get a nibble and he wouldn't care. My dad worked hard and long and never complained.

The only job I remember my mom having was a carhop. At first she worked at Theo's Drive In (similar to Sonic) in Grand Prairie. I remember that so well because it was right next to a Goodwill store and we loved going to Goodwill, where they sold used clothes, shoes, and furniture. This store was our Neiman Marcus. Because, believe me, anything they had in there was a lot better than what we had. After Theo's, my mom worked at the old A&W Root Beer as a carhop. She used to bring home onion rings and French fries that were left over from her shift. We thought this was the greatest job in the world, all the French fries and onion rings you could eat. What could be better than that?

CHAPTER 5

On The Move, Again

WE MOVED AROUND quite a bit when I was little. The first house I remember us living in was just outside of Grand Prairie in a community call Lake View. I remember this house because of the lake. I was about five years old. We could walk down the road and be at the lake. It wasn't a nice lake by any means; in fact I think it was a manmade lake to support the electricity plant on the other side. There was always lots of trash and stuff floating in it. I don't know that any of us knew how to swim, but we would go there to play. It was pretty sad the day we had to move away from the lake.

The next place we lived was an apartment complex somewhere in Grand Prairie; we just called it the pink apartments because the building was pink. The thing I remember about the apartments is the day we came home and were locked out. My dad told me to go around and crawl through the window and unlock the front door. Well, I shot out around the back but I was somewhat distracted. One of the other neighborhood boys was holding a stick, threatening another boy, and the boy holding the stick asked me to hold the stick while

ON THE MOVE, AGAIN

he went to get his dad, so of course I said okay. The next thing I remember is a tremendous smack on my rear end. Of course it was my dad; apparently I had been holding the stick for at least ten minutes and had forgotten all about unlocking the door. To this day my dad is still mad about that day because he broke his watch, which was the best watch he ever owned. I was never told, but putting two and two together, I realized the reason the door was locked was because we were getting kicked out. My dad went to get my uncle Melvin and you would be impressed with how fast eight or nine kids and a couple of grownups can clear out an entire apartment full of furniture and stuff.

The next place we lived was in Mansfield, Texas. This was about 1969 because I was just starting the first grade. Mansfield had eight to ten thousand people at the time. This is where I really start to remember events and things that happened and how they affected my family and me. Mansfield was your typical small Texas town, with a small grocery store called Lee's Super Market, a Gibson's department store, a Western Auto, a 7-Eleven and of course a Dairy Queen. As of today that Dairy Queen is still in operation. Mansfield had two elementary schools, Erma Nash and Alice Ponder, a middle school (sixth grade), a junior high, and a high school.

We lived in a two-story wood frame house in town and, as always, the house was old and run down. We didn't use the upstairs during the winter because it was too cold; remember, no heat or air-conditioning. The house was on a corner with a pretty good-size yard and lots of trees. The front porch was about twenty feet long across the front of the house with a roof covering the whole thing. From the bedrooms we could crawl out the windows and play on the porch cover. It was only about eight feet off the ground, so it made a perfect launch pad to the ground. The most fun we ever had in this house was when Andy and Jerry found a couple of huge pieces of foam rubber that we used for several weeks. The game was simple: jump off the porch cover onto the foam doing whatever flips, trick, or whatever you thought you could do and not get killed.

We lived about one mile from Erma Nash Elementary School so we walked most of the time. First grade was great; in fact I remember thinking school was great for a time. We got to eat lunch every day and we got to take naps (or at least I did, in the first grade). First grade was also great because I wanted to marry my teacher, Ms. Argo. No disrespect to any other women in my life...Momma, aunts or my granny, but Mrs. Argo was the first real lady I ever really spent any time with. She was very petite with dark hair and real nice. I never heard a cuss word come out of her mouth, she never told anyone to shut up, and she never smacked anyone. She probably didn't have any kids at home and as a result maintained her "perfect lady" status.

Mr. Glenn Harmon was the principal at Erma Nash. In fact he was the principal when my oldest brother Rocky went to school there, all the way down to when my youngest sisters went to school. Mr. Harmon was another one of those people who really helped our family a lot. I think he would make sure our name was on as many "help needed" lists as he could find. Mr. Harmon was a big man, but was generally very soft-spoken and caring. In a small town like Mansfield, I am sure the principal knows every student and most of the parents by

ON THE MOVE, AGAIN

name, but it always seemed as if Mr. Harmon looked out for us and went out of his way to help our family.

There are several things that happened during our time in this house that stand out in my mind. Not that they were life-altering or anything like that but more of a realization of what family really meant. It was the first time that I can remember realizing our place in society's hierarchy.

When you are a kid (under six years old) you never think about where food comes from or what clothes you wear or where your dad works; all you know is playing, getting in trouble, or trying not to get in trouble and the proverbial "Don't be last so you are not the rotten egg." During my first week of first grade I realized that I was one of the Conn kids. I found this out from Ms. Argo. In those days the teacher would collect your lunch money in the morning. When she called my name to bring her my lunch money the first couple of days, her response, when I got to her desk with no money was, "You are one of the Conn kids, right?" Of course being from Texas I just said, "Yes, ma'am." It was only a week or so later that Kathleen Russell (the self-appointed social chair of first grade) informed me that I must be poor, and that's why I got free lunches. I saw the other kids either paying Ms. Argo or saying out loud, "I brought my lunch," so I'm not sure why it didn't register in my mind that I didn't actually have to pay for lunch. I don't think it really bothered me but I remember asking my brothers on the way home that afternoon if they got free lunches at school and they of course said, "Yes." When you hear things about your family from other people it is easy to think they don't know what they are talking about, or they are just being mean. However, when you actually hear it from members of your own family, you realize it must be true. When I asked them why we got free lunches I remember Andy stopping dead in his tracks right in front of the big church bell and looking right at me to say, "Because we are poor, you dummy!" I never had to pay for my lunch at school, nor did my sisters or brothers who followed me. I'm sure other kids got free lunches too, but my family never even had to fill out the paperwork, because we were part of the Conn Family. Everyone knew we were poor.

Things began to add up over the next year or so, things that may otherwise have gone unnoticed to a young boy. Realizing that you are poor at six or seven years old helps you understand the way some things happen. I didn't necessarily understand at the time but later when I looked back, things just made sense. Things like shopping at Goodwill. I thought Goodwill was the store where you bought clothes, furniture, shoes, and stuff. It was a department store, not a store that you go to when you are poor. I didn't know the things we bought there were the things other people were throwing away; it was just the store we shopped when we really needed something. Coming home and being locked out of your house or apartment and staying with aunts and uncles for a week or so until you get another house, driving around in my dad's truck picking up furniture and stuff from people to put in your new house, things start making sense.

Anyway, the house in Mansfield was pretty cool for us kids. There were lots of kids on our street and a couple of families that were almost as large as ours. The Moerickes lived down the street and I think they had six or seven kids, and the Heath family lived a little further down and I think they had seven

ON THE MOVE, AGAIN

or eight kids. Rusty Braswell was the coolest kid on the block. He lived across the street with his mom, dad, and sister. His dad was pretty cool too. He had several coon dogs that he took hunting on many occasions. I got to go with them once and it was pretty amazing watching those dogs tree a raccoon. Then Rusty's dad would come over and shoot it. There was always something going on and always something to do. Things that didn't cost money. When you can't afford to pay for extracurricular activities, you find things that don't cost money to occupy your time.

So I found out about a boxing team in Mansfield and I started boxing with them soon after we moved in. The coach had a son about two years older than me and as I recall there were twelve to fifteen boys of various ages training in his garage. We would run through the cemetery as part of our training and I hated it. I was always scared to go through the cemetery at night, but it made me run faster. We never had the money to join things like the Scouts or other clubs or activities, but Jim didn't charge us anything for the boxing lessons, so I got to do that for a while. I remember Jim always had a small life lesson that he would tell us after each boxing lesson. His point was always respect your competition, respect adults, and always without fail, respect your parents.

Respecting my mom was never an issue; she was a no-nonsense kind of parent. When she said something she meant it literally and we all knew it. One Christmas, our uncle Dale gave three of the boys a BB gun. That is one gun to share among the three of us...it was the Winchester-style rifle with the long steel barrel and a wood handle. It was so cool! Momma's only real rule was "Don't shoot anybody!" Well, how were we supposed to know that rule meant even one accident? We were all in the front yard shooting at something and one of the BBs ricocheted off something and hit Sissy in the face. We knew the blood-curdling scream would have Momma coming outside any minute, so we all tried consoling her, begging her to stop crying, but it didn't work. Momma stepped out the front door and just looked at the situation, held her hand out, and with just one action, she was the judge, the jury, and the executioner. It only took about ten seconds for her to beat that gun on the concrete porch until it was in a hundred pieces. She didn't say anything and we didn't say anything; we knew what would happen if someone got hit with a BB. Well, it was fun while it lasted. While we accepted the punishment we didn't agree with it.

One thing that must be upheld in the hierarchy of siblings is payback. We still to this day don't think Sissy was hurt that bad, but she knew Momma would either take our gun or spank all of us and that is why she screamed and cried so much that day. So to make sure she understood the magnitude of her action, we had to retaliate with something of hers. The next day, we put her favorite doll in the oven and burned it up. Of course we all got a good spanking for it, but the message was sent and we were all even.

The realization of being poor hit home a couple more times during that next year or two. We never had frivolous types of food in our house, like cupcakes, soda, candy, fruit, or snacks in general. We ate toast or maybe oatmeal for breakfast, we ate lunch at school, and for dinner the usual red beans and taters. We never had a lot but we always seemed to have some. But as I was getting a bit older and was now included in some of

ON THE MOVE, AGAIN

the things that I was not included in just a few months earlier, I learned that things I shrugged off as "oh well" now were making a bit more sense. I never asked "why" when a couple of my older brothers didn't eat dinner before; it wasn't my business and I didn't care. I was eating. Well, now it makes sense.

I remember the day my mom called all four of us boys into the house and asked if we would skip dinner so the little ones could eat. As a child I don't ever remember my mom crying until that day. I didn't know what to think but I remember Rocky stepping up real quick, telling her that we weren't even hungry anyway, and he ushered us all back outside. I was the last to leave and remember my mom smiling at me through her tears. I asked Rocky, once we were back outside, why he told Momma we weren't hungry. He just said, "It ain't the first time we don't eat and you're big enough to not eat today; besides, that means we can play more. We can eat tomorrow."

As a family that never went to church, we never had a "God does everything for a reason" or "God will provide" moment in our family. We had what we had and we got by. By the same token, my dad never made excuses and never blamed anyone or anything for our family situation. He just worked hard every day and gave us the best he could. Looking back at all of the things that could have gone really bad for us, I realize now there is no doubt God was watching over the family.

That next afternoon, Andy and I were walking down the street toward the Moerickes' house and I saw something slowly moving across the street. As I ran to pick it up, I almost fell over, because it was ten-dollar bill! I told (yelled to) Andy,

"Hey, look, it's money," and as he came running up to me he called me a liar. I held it up to show him and he snatched it out of my hand and started running back home. Andy was really fast so he got there at least two or three minutes before me. I was crying by the time I got home because I wanted to be the one to give it to Momma. I found it and I should have the glory. When I walked in, Momma was already getting her shoes on and said she would be right back. She was going to the store. Everyone was yelling, "Can I go? Can I go?" Momma yelled out, "Y'all stop it, ain't none of you goin'. Just stay here, I will be right back!" I remember we had fried pork chops and macaroni and cheese and Kool-Aid with sugar in it that night with our beans and it was really good. Nobody believed me when I said that I was the one who found the money, nobody but Momma that is. While we were all getting ready for bed, Momma came in to make sure everyone was calming down, and she leaned over and very quietly whispered in my ear, "Thanks for supper." It was truly one of the best days of my life.

Even though we only lived there for a short time, a lot happened that shaped the way I looked at our family and more importantly the way I looked at how other people saw us. This was about the time that I realized Santa didn't bring toys at Christmastime; churches did, and they also brought food and clothes. It was the first time I remember people coming to our house during the holidays with toys, food, and clothes. I never knew why we had to move from that house but memories of the landlord coming to our house every week probably meant that we couldn't pay the rent, so we moved to a house in Webb, Texas.

CHAPTER 6

The Summer Of 1971

WEBB, WHICH IS located just south of Arlington, nestled between Dallas and Ft. Worth, Texas, was your typical Andy Griffith type of town. The downtown part was made up of fifty or sixty houses on eight streets. Everyone knew everyone, no traffic lights, and the main industry was a cotton gin. There was a feed store and I think a real estate or insurance office, I can't remember which one. There was only one church, and of course being in the south it was a Baptist church. We had a volunteer fire department with one fire truck, no police, and no post office. We had one grocery store called Dorsey's. Mr. and Mrs. Dorsey lived in the back of the store. They owned it until they got too old to run it. The two gas pumps were the kind where you had to turn the crank to reset the pump; they carried the basic grocery items, some meats, produce, and your basic sundry items. I am sure most people paid cash for their groceries, but we didn't; we charged them and then paid what we could when Daddy got paid. I don't know but I'm pretty sure we still owe the Dorseys some money. We actually lived about a mile and a half down the road from the center of town. There was a small trailer park across the street from us and there were three other houses on the one-and-a-half-mile road that we lived on.

Everything around us was either cotton fields, hay fields, or grazing pastures for the cows. There was always a small field of corn or some other crop but mainly hay or cotton. We lived at Rural Route 3, Box 351. The house we lived in was your typical fifty-year-old farmhouse. It was wood frame with no heat or air-conditioning. We couldn't drink the water from the faucet because of the rusty pipes that brought the water from the well. We had to get our drinking water from Dorsey's store. Every couple of days, we would either pull the wagon down the mile road to fill up the five-gallon jug, or if the weather was bad we would drive down. This house was actually a pretty big house as compared to what we would live in for the next ten years. This house had three bedrooms, a living room, and a kitchen/dining room. There were no hallways, just one room opening into the next room.

The landlord, Mr. English, raised cows, lots of cows. We had a pretty good-size lot where we raised a few chickens, a couple of goats, and even the occasional rabbit. Most of the stuff we raised was to eat or sell. We didn't really have pets. I remember one of my daddy's sayings, "If you can't eat it, you don't need it!" We also had a small garden where we grew some vegetables, never a lot of anything, just some stuff we ate. The best thing about this house was our swimming pool. Well, kind of. There was a cow trough next to our house that we would use for swimming. As a child I remember it being huge. In actuality, it was only about two and a half feet deep, about twelve feet across, and maybe twenty feet long. I remember it being an Olympic-size pool. Again, looking back, it was really disgusting. There were eight inches of moss on the bottom, the water of course was green, there was slime on all of the walls, but at the time, it was a great swimming pool.

Webb was a tight-knit community with mainly older people, and only a few families with kids young enough to be in school. Everyone rode the bus to school and most of us just met at Dorsey's store, the local bus stop. My new best friend in Webb was Daniel. His family lived in a small trailer house next door to Dorsey's store. He had one brother and one sister, his mom didn't work, and his dad worked but went to college at night. I loved being at Daniel's house because his mom always did neat stuff, like put Kool-Aid in the ice trays and make homemade popsicles. They were kind of a weird family though. One night I was invited to stay for dinner; however, I didn't stay because they were having goat's head. It was real goat's head that had been cooked in the oven like a roast or something and they ate it right off the head. I went home and told my family about it and most of them said I was a liar. This was another one of those times when you realize that it is sometimes better not to know something. So I decided to hurry home and have the old faithful, beans and taters, for dinner. When I got home, I was pleasantly surprised and very happy with my decision.

My mom had cooked what we thought was chicken for dinner that night. As my brothers and I were grossing out over the goat head story, my mom said, "Well, what do you think you are eating for dinner tonight?" The overwhelming response was "chicken." Momma smiled and said, "No, it is armadillo." Of course we all laughed and said she was just teasing us. Momma then said, "Well, why don't you go out back and look in the trash can and tell me what you see." We all ran out the back door and looked in the trash can and saw a big armadillo shell. Apparently, Daddy saw this thing in our garden and shot it, so Momma skinned it and fried it up like a chicken. Jerry was kind of sick but the rest of us considered it a great day because we were having meat for dinner. Daddy didn't say a word, but I remember this grin on his face that made me smile. He thought it was pretty funny.

I think about the things my dad taught us by his words and by his actions, and a few things always stand out. His belief that you make do with what you have, be thankful for what you have, and, the biggest, don't complain about what you don't have. He was a simple man who accepted his life, did the best he could, worked hard for what he had, and was never envious of others. But then there were things that we did as a family that I think were kind of hypocritical. My dad would beat your ass with a belt, his hand, or a boot if you ever stole something. I remember during this time, the biggest thing in the world was mood rings. Everyone at school had them; they were so cool and only cost like two dollars. Of course no one in our family had one, because they cost two dollars. Then one day one of the girls noticed that Jerry had one on his finger. Well, as soon as my dad got home, the investigation began. It only took about two minutes of questioning and Jerry admitted that he took the ring from a girl's desk at school. After the brief ass-whipping, the true punishment was announced. Jerry would take the ring back to school tomorrow, give it to Mr. Harmon, the principal, tell him who the ring belonged to, and have Mr. Harmon write a note that would be brought back to Momma, confirming the return of the ring. Then his at-home punishment would be doing the dishes by himself for the next week. While the punishment seemed fair because we don't take stuff that is not ours, it contradicts what I learned just a few months earlier. This was the first time I ever participated, and I guess it may have happened before, but again, I may have been too young. My mom loaded us all up in the car and drove to the Gibson's department store in Grand Prairie, I remember it being Grand Prairie because I asked Andy why we would go all the way to Grand Prairie when there was a Gibson's in Mansfield, which was a lot closer. He just said, "This one is the best one." As we are driving Momma told us to take off our socks and shoes. When Momma tells you something you don't usually ask questions, you just do it. So I did. So my mom pulls up to the front of the store and says, "Okay, boys, I want each of you to go inside and put on a pair of tennis shoes that fit and then hurry back out here, no playing around." So as we all hopped out, Momma yelled to Rocky, "You help John Darrel." Without even looking back or slowing down, Rocky yelled back, "Yes, ma'am." We all headed in and straight to the boys' shoe department. Andy, Jerry, and Rocky all quickly put on a pair of shoes, and then Rocky grabbed a pair of shoes, yanked me to the floor, slipped the shoes on my feet, and said, "Do they fit?" I stood up and said yeah. He grabbed my arm and said, "Okay, let's go." We walked quickly out of the store and there was Momma sitting out front. We all hopped in the car and headed home.

Now, I am not a police officer or a lawyer or a judge, but I think by most accounts, what we did was stealing. Momma explained on the way home that these shoes were for school, not for after school. "When you get home, you take them off and wear you old ones for after-school stuff." That is all that was said. No explanations, no questions, nothing. We needed shoes; now we had shoes.

Food seemed to be another item that was okay for the taking. There were several occasions that Momma would drop us off next to corn fields with a pillow case in hand and our job was to go a little ways into the field, fill the pillow case with corn, and when yours was full, you made your way back to the street and waved. Momma would pull up and you got in the car. After everyone was back in the car, we would go home with a huge haul of fresh corn. Again, I think most people would consider this stealing. Obviously, there is a difference between stealing a mood ring and a necessity like shoes and food. We never questioned our actions; we just did what we did, right or wrong.

The rest of this year went by without anything significant happening that I am aware. We were all getting older. Trisha was almost two, Jaimie must have been around three, Sherrill was four, Sissy was starting kindergarten, I was going to second grade, Jerry was in the fourth, and Andy was moving out of elementary school into the sixth grade. Rocky was big time because he was about to finish junior high.

This year was relatively quiet, with just a few affirmations of things I learned in first grade and second grade. I remember one time when a magician was going to perform at the school and the cost was a dime per student. As I recall, it was for all grades, because Jerry and I had a plan to ask Mom for the money. I went to her the day before the assembly and said, "Momma, there is this thing tomorrow at school and it is free…for only a dime." Well, anyway, to make a short story

THE SUMMER OF 1971

even shorter, we didn't go. The affirmation I am talking about is this: The students who didn't want to attend or couldn't afford to attend events or shows went to the library during the assembly. The only kids in the library that day were me, Jerry, Sissy, a girl named Beth, and her sister. I don't know Beth's financial situation at home but she and her sister were very smart and I think they would rather spend the time reading than watching a magician. As I look back on that day, it makes me realize just how poor we really were. People who say they were poor but just didn't know it weren't really poor! We were poor and we definitely knew it.

This was also about the time that I got to go with the older kids to the U.S. cold storage in Grand Prairie. This was a large facility that was owned and operated by some department of the government that distributed or held food for various reasons. I remember going there for the first time to get cheese, big blocks of "government cheese." You had to stand in line and when it was your turn, they simply handed you a huge block of cheddar cheese, weighing around seven pounds; it may have been a lot less, but since I was only five years old, it seemed huge. You were only allowed a certain amount, but that is why Momma took several of us. She would get in line with Sissy, but Rocky would get in line further back and stand there with me and then Andy and Jerry would get in line somewhere else, so we would get three rations of cheese. Sometimes we would get big boxes of powdered milk that you just added water to, to make somewhat of a milk product. There may have been other items you could get, but I just remember the cheese, big, huge blocks of cheese. Anything free was good and we sure accepted it.

RED BEANS & TATERS

I don't know if this was true in first and second grade and I just don't remember or if it started in third grade, but Friday was the best day at school because it was free ice cream day at lunch. You could buy an ice cream any day, but it did not come with the "free lunch." However, on Friday, the lunch lady would push a big pan of assorted ice creams down the middle of the table and everyone got one. I loved free ice cream day.

The summer of 1971 was also my introduction to church. I started going to church in Mansfield at the First Baptist Church. I forget who invited me; I think it was Brad Faulkner. Anyway, the Sunday school teacher would drive all the way out to our house and pick me up for Sunday school and church and then take me back home. I remember feeling a bit out of place because I didn't know very much about church or the Bible or anything that went along with religion. In a typical defensive stance, I remember getting a lot of flak and razzing from my family about going to church. You know, stuff like, "You think you're better than us 'cause you go to church" and "Why don't you get God to send home a new TV or some food?" This was mainly from my older brothers. Momma thought it was good and encouraged me to go. Sunday school was a small escape from my family; there was no fighting, yelling, cussing, just a bunch of kids my own age sitting in a circle talking about stuff. I don't remember a whole lot of specific things about Sunday school but I do remember a few special days.

The first one I remember is when we all came into class and sat down; then our teacher looked at us and said, "How many of you got up this morning and told your dad you loved him?" After the question was asked, without even thinking about

THE SUMMER OF 1971

it I said, "Why?" I remember the whole class looking at me and the teacher said, "Well, John, you should always tell your parents that you love them but today is a special day. It is Fathers' Day." I remember this day because it was the first time I realized that no one in my family ever said *I love you* to anyone else in the family. We never celebrated Mother's Day, or Father's Day and in fact, I don't ever remember ever celebrating a birthday. No cakes, no parties.

Learning about God and the Bible should have been the focal point of my going to church and Sunday school but for me it was an opportunity to be with other kids that summer and not just my siblings. Church was a quiet and peaceful place. Another special time I have always remembered was when my Sunday school teacher, Larry, promised that anyone who memorized the books of the Bible (Old and New Testament) would be invited to his house for a hamburger cookout, so you better believe that I learned them. That Sunday afternoon at my Sunday school teacher's house, we played games and we ate. There was more food than I had ever seen and I could eat as much as I wanted. I remember thinking this was one of the best days of my life. Again, not that my family was horrible or anything; it was just the simple fact that we were not your typical family.

Our summers were filled with lots of outside stuff, like playing, fighting, football, more fighting, make-believe, and then more fighting. We didn't have lots of toys to play with so we played a lot of football, army, and make-believe. One of our favorite things to do was build a city in the dirt. We would spend hours making the roads and building fences around the property. Of course you had to go find your own rocks for your house and twigs for your fences. It was great because we got to have a big house with lots of land. You could own the store or the bank or whatever you wanted. The game never lasted very long after the city was built. I think the fun was just building.

Saturday morning cartoons were something all kids looked forward to, and we were no different. Who doesn't remember the commercials on Saturday morning, things like "Conjunction Junction, What's your function?" and "I'm just a bill." We would spend several hours watching until the discussion about what we were watching next became more than a discussion. Momma would intervene and send us all outside or make us clean the house or something.

Our evenings for the most part were spent in front of the television when we had one and it was working. There were only three major television channels back then but there were two local channels. For as many years as I can remember we watched *Gilligan's Island, I Love Lucy, Dick Van Dyke, Beverly Hillbillies, Gunsmoke, Rifleman* and *Perry Mason*. That was pretty much the extent of TV shows. Saturday nights were the best because we watched the country and western variety shows. There was *Hee Haw, The Grand Ole Opry, The Porter Wagoner Show, Laredo* and then the thing that we looked forward to the most was *Saturday Night Wrestling*. Fritz Von Erich was the king every Saturday night at 10:00. As fake as wrestling is today, it does not compare to the early days. Sunday was pretty much the same as Saturday but we would almost always watch *The Wonderful World of Disney* movie in the evening. This was as close to family time as we had. I can still see five or six kids lying on the floor, Daddy sitting in his chair, and Momma on the couch holding a baby. There always seemed to be a baby in the house and there also always seemed to be another family at our house on the weekends.

Three of my mom's brothers and one of her sisters lived close by and always ended up at our house with their kids. The men would always be working on someone's car and the women would usually be sitting in the house and all of the kids playing in the yard. A special day would be a trip to the flea market in Kennedale. We never really bought anything but it was fun to go and look at all of the stuff. Daddy might buy a couple of chickens or something like that, but mainly it was a day away from the house.

The start of the school year was usually a great time for everyone in the family. It meant Momma wouldn't have seven or eight kids at home all day. It meant lower food bills at home because we would all eat lunch at school and it meant less fighting at home because we wouldn't all be on each other's nerves and in each other's business.

I remember the bus ride to school because it was exciting. We had to walk about a mile from our house to the bus stop in Webb. I had never ridden a school bus. When we first moved to Webb, riding the bus was just a way to get to school but soon it became another place that I would meet someone who made a huge impact on my life. We didn't have assigned seats or anything like that, unless of course you misbehaved and the bus driver made you sit in the first seat so he could keep an eye on you. Typically the order of the bus went by grade. The elementary school kids sat in the front section, the junior high school kids sat in the middle section, and the high school kids sat in the back section. Everyone who rode the bus knew everyone else and most people pretty much sat in the same old place.

Mr. Horace Howard was the bus driver. He was a retired senior citizen who started driving a school bus to keep busy. I found out really quick that Mr. Howard also was a member of the Mansfield First Baptist Church, which happened to be the church I had just started attending. He was not bashful about talking to people about going to church and doing good things for one another. After just a few weeks of riding the bus, Mr. Howard and I became good friends. He said one time to keep me in line I had to sit up front just to the left of the driver's seat. Actually, what I got to do was push the signal button that turned on the flashing yellow lights, indicating that the bus was about to stop and then I would push the other button that turned on the red lights, indicating that the bus would stop. I thought this was pretty cool because no else got to do it. During most of the bus ride Mr. Howard would talk to me about everyday stuff, but sometimes he would go into a small lesson about getting an education, being nice to my brothers and sisters, and the most frequent conversation was about helping out around the house. Mr. Howard was always nice to everyone, but he was especially nice to our family. The First Baptist Church of Mansfield soon became a big supporter of the Conn family. They brought us food, clothes, and at Christmastime, they brought us presents. Other churches and groups would bring stuff to us but it seemed the Mansfield First Baptist Church brought the most stuff and the most often. I definitely think Mr. Howard was the driving force behind the church's gifts. He was another one of those people who went out of his way to make sure he either taught me something or made sure I understood something that would benefit me later in life. Of course it wasn't then but it is now quite obvious to me.

Maybe Mr. Howard had these little talks with my brothers and other kids on the bus and I just never noticed. He would quiz me on the books of the Bible, or tell me to tuck my shirt in and look presentable. He always asked me to tell him something I learned at school that day and he always asked how my mom was doing. The thing I try to keep with me that I learned from Mr. Howard is to care for or at least be nice to everyone. I know that I haven't always done that, but I think it made a difference in the way I live my life as an adult.

CHAPTER 7

Back to the Story

SO MOMMA GOT out of the car with the new baby; it was August 11th 1971. I don't know exactly but since Shelly was born on August 8th, I figure it was two or three days after that. I was eight years old then and about to start the third grade. Nothing out of the ordinary about Shelly; after all, Momma had already done this nine other times. She was born at the county hospital in Dallas and everything seemed to have been just fine. Everything went back to normal just a few days later. In fact the next six or eight months were relatively quiet around our house except for the occasional fight between brothers.

It's funny how stuff rolls downhill. Being the youngest of the big boys I always had to rely on protection from one of the bigger brothers. So if Jerry started a fight with me then of course Andy had to step in. So it was the domino effect. If Jerry hit me then Andy would hit him and then of course Rocky would hit Andy. The bad side to this was that I didn't get to hit anyone and Rocky never got hit, but it probably worked out even in the end.

BACK TO THE STORY

So here we are, August of 1971. Rocky is fourteen going on fifteen years old, in high school, playing football and the coronet in the high school band. Andy is thirteen, in junior high doing whatever junior high school kids do. Jerry, Sissy and I are still in elementary school. She is in the first grade. Robert is nine years old and still living with Herschel. Sherrill is five and will start school the following year. Jaimie is four years old and the apple of my daddy's eye. Trisha is two or so and Shelly is now the baby.

The makeup of our family is kind of strange when you look at the many different features and characteristics among the kids. I understand the basic genetic thing and how some genes may dominate in one child but not another and I'm sure the more children in a family the more opportunities for various characteristics, but ours seemed to be very widespread. Rocky was a pretty big boy with black curly hair who would eventually grow to be six feet, two inches tall. He seemed to be more mature than his age from a physical standpoint. He always tried to be the leader of the boys, but he never really had the leadership qualities. He was more of the muscle—bullheaded and stubborn and not afraid to mix it up, if necessary.

Then there was Andy, who was just a biscuit over five-foot-seven, with blond hair. Andy is probably the smartest of the bunch and was actually very athletic for being somewhat small. He is also the most gifted in the art department. We used to sit and marvel at his artistic ability. Freelance drawing was his specialty. He could draw most anything, but horse and scenic views were his specialty. Andy was very diplomatic; he always seemed to be the one trying to reason with everyone.

Next was Jerry. He was more of the "whatever" type person. He was tall and skinny with brownish-blond hair. School was never his idea of a good time. If someone had to be labeled the troublemaker in every group, Jerry would be ours. Not that he was a bad kid, but more so that he didn't mind challenging authority or trying to get around it when possible. Jerry would end up at just over six feet tall and always skinny.

Even though Robert wasn't around the rest of us growing up, he was still a brother. I think the fact that he may have eaten a little better, meaning he had a proper diet and stuff like that, may have contributed to his physical nature. At the age of thirteen or fourteen Robert stood over six feet tall and weighed over a hundred and sixty pounds. Robert and Jerry shared many facial features and hair color, but Robert's bone structure and weight were far beyond any of the rest of us. In fact, Robert topped out at about six foot six, and weighed over two hundred and fifty pounds.

Me, well, I was closer to Andy from a physical standpoint. Somewhat short and skinny with blond hair, I was considered by my older brothers to be a Momma's boy, but I think it was just because I was the youngest and the smallest. You had to be tough to live in our house, but after a while even the tough kids had enough. So when I was tired of being picked on or held down and being red-bellied, then I would seek the protection of a mightier warrior, Mom.

At an early age, it was obvious that Sissy was going to be a lot like Momma. She was never fat, but always a little heavy. Pawpaw used to say that she was just big boned. Sissy has dark brown hair and brown eyes, with a dark complexion just like Momma. She was tough like the boys and she could hold her own in any fight.

Sherrill was always petite. She had very blonde hair and a very light complexion. She was the female version of Jerry. Not a bad child but always seemed to the one getting caught or at least blamed for stuff.

Jamie was the spitting image of Billie Harris. He had dark hair and even had the same (although less pronounced) speech impediment. I think he probably had speech services through the school system because as he got older, the impediment seemed to be less obvious. The only difference between Jamie and Daddy was that Jamie would end up being taller, somewhere around the six feet, one inch area.

Patricia looked a lot like Sherrill (giving a little more credibility to the story of who Sherrill's father is). White blonde hair, a few freckles, and light complexion. Trisha was more outgoing and didn't seem to get in as much trouble as Sherrill.

Finally, there was Shelly. The only redheaded child in the whole bunch and lots of freckles. Shelly would turn out to be about the same height and everything as Sherrill and Trisha but would never lose the red hair or the freckles.

Everyone was adjusting to the baby. School was starting soon and things seemed to be back to normal. Daddy was still working at the gas station in Grand Prairie and Momma stayed home with the kids.

CHAPTER 8

Fall Of '71

THIRD GRADE WOULD turn out to be a great year at school for me. Joe Holman and Joey Davis entered my life and would have a great effect on me during the school year and for years to come.

Joe Holman, whom I didn't like in second grade, was immediately my new best friend. I don't know why he became my best friend; it just happened. We were in different homeroom classes, but we had several subject classes together.

Joe's family was a bit like mine but not quite to our level. His mom and dad were both somewhat educated, meaning they finished high school, and I think his dad had some college. Janice and Jack Holman (after a while I just called them Mom and Dad). They were like adopted parents. Joe had two brothers, Wade and Bryan, and one sister, Suzanne. Joe was the baby. They didn't have a lot but when you only have four kids to share with, having a little seems like a lot to someone with nine brothers and sisters.

FALL OF '71

Joe's dad was a construction foreman and his mom was a stay-at-home mom. They lived just outside of Mansfield in a trailer house with a room added on; that was the boys' bedroom. Mom, Dad, and Suzanne had the two bedrooms in the trailer. One of the great things about Joe's house was the land. They had about two acres of land that they used to raise a couple of cows and Suzanne always had a horse. They raised the cows for beef. As I mentioned earlier, they always had meat; every night for dinner they had meat. The big joke for a long time was that every time I came over to spend the night, they had hamburgers. The others complained but I was just happy to have meat, so I was good with it.

Mom and Dad always treated me like a son. They even bought me a toothbrush and made me brush my teeth when I was at their house. I loved going over to Joe's house. It was like the families you see on television. Mom and Dad sitting in their chairs reading books, a couple of kids lying on the floor watching television together, and maybe a couple of kids at the table playing a game. The house was warm (literally) in the wintertime and cool in the summer. They always said a prayer before supper and they all drank milk with dinner.

Wade and Bryan were like any other brothers, though. They picked on us all the time, beat us when they wanted to, held us down and farted on our heads and other fun stuff that big brothers do. Wade was about sixteen or so when Joe and I became friends. I remember him driving so he had to be at least sixteen or seventeen. Bryan was fourteen or fifteen, and Suzanne was thirteen. Suzanne was such a tomboy that it seemed as though Joe had three brothers.

Joe and I developed a friendship that most people only dream about. Again, I don't know how or why we bonded the way we did, but it was simply meant to be. We would go through the next ten or twelve years as absolutely the best friends anyone could possibly imagine. We played during school, spent the night at each other's house on the weekends, and spent almost the entire summer together. We went through the joys of moving on to junior high and high school; we cried together over broken hearts and scraped knees. We shared the deepest and most sacred of secrets together. Nothing was kept from one another.

Joe's mom treated me like one of her own. When I was there, I had chores just like everyone else, but I didn't mind. The tradeoff of having her motherly wisdom was worth it. She bought me my first can of deodorant and explained to me and Joe that we were not little boys anymore and that we stink, so we needed to start taking care of our own hygiene.

Joey Davis was another situation where I don't remember how or why we hooked up as friends, but we just did. Joey was your typical kid except that it seems like he was always taller than everyone else in the class. Maybe it was just me being short. Joey had three sisters, two older than him and one younger. The older sisters were Laurie and Valarie and his younger sister was Stacy. Joey's dad died when he was young and his mother married Eugene. Like me and Billie Harris, I have never heard Joey call Eugene anything but Dad. Eugene was a very quiet man much like my dad, but he was larger than life. Physically, he was very tall and husky with a very deep voice. I was never scared of Mr. Parker, but was always in awe of him. He had a presence that commanded respect. He never said much to me but when he spoke, I listened.

Mrs. Parker was one of the room mothers for our class in third grade. I'm sure there were other room moms but I can't recall who they were. I just remember Mrs. Parker. She was very soft-spoken and always had a very kind tone to her voice, except when we were in trouble and she used your middle name... you know, the one that makes you stop in your tracks and tuck tail. She was the "picture perfect" mom. To me, room moms were so cool. They brought stuff to all our parties, they always seemed to be around the school, and everyone knew them and everyone knew it was your mom. I remember asking my mom one time why she wasn't a room mom and she simply said, "I have nine kids of my own to take care of. Why would I want to be a mom to twenty more that aren't even mine?" or something of that nature. Regardless, I got the point. I am sure we had parties and stuff in first and second grade, but I don't remember them like the ones we had in third grade.

It is hard to have a social life in elementary school when you live fifteen miles out of town, you have eight brothers and sisters living with you, your dad works all the time, and your family only has one car. But for every situation like this, there is a Barbara Parker to the rescue.

The in-crowd was attending a birthday party for Rhonda at the skating rink in Rendon and I was invited. The only problem was getting there. This was the first in a long list of the times that Mrs. Parker helped me out. I don't know that Joey and I were such good friends that he would have invited me over to spend the night after the skating party, so I think his mom may have persuaded him a little bit. But regardless I was going to spend the night at Joey's house. Everything was great, except that I had never been skating before and didn't know how. But hey, when you are in third grade you can do anything, right?

I remember that skating party so well, the lights, and the music, me inching along the edge of the wall. I think it took me fifteen minutes to go around each time. But I didn't care. It didn't take long until I was getting pretty good at skating. Soon I was actually skating without holding onto the walls. I am sure I had several falls and trips and crashes but the only one I remember is the big one. Feeling good about myself and my skating abilities, I entered one of the races. Going good, made the first two turns okay, in last place, but still standing, and then the turns three and four, no problem, building speed. The hardest thing about going fast on skates when you are just learning to skate is the stopping part. So I busted big time. I don't remember what I hit or how I hit it but it was hard. There was no blood or cuts or anything like that, just a very badly busted, bruised and black eye. The thing about this story is what happened after we got back to Joey's house. I guess the eye must have been pretty bad because Mrs. Parker sat beside my bed all night. Not just for a while until I went to sleep, but all night. I think most moms would have taken me home and let my mom deal with it. But not Mrs. Parker. She replaced my ice pack or cold rag whatever it was all night long. Even with the end result, this was one of my favorite memories of elementary school. Of course the next day at school everyone knew that I couldn't skate and everyone wanted to see my eye, but all of that was okay because for just a day or two I was very popular.

FALL OF '71

To this day, I can't look at a moon pie without thinking of Joey and Mrs. Parker and all of the things they did for me over the years. In third grade, I think our lunchtime must have been later in the day, because we had a snack time, in the middle of the morning. Of course I didn't bring anything for snack because we didn't have things at home to bring. I don't remember how or when it started but one day Joey happened to have two moon pies for snack that day and he gave one to me. I remember thinking that moon pies rated right up there with free ice-cream day in the lunchroom. Sometimes it would be the chocolate one and sometimes it would be the vanilla one. It didn't matter to me. At the young age of fifty, Joey and I still talk about the moon pie. His mom made him bring me a moon pie even during a time when he was either mad at me or I was mad at him or he didn't like me, but he always brought the moon pie and I always accepted it.

Another one of my dad's great sayings was "Don't be proud; pride won't fill your stomach." Daddy would never ask for a handout or a free meal or anything like that, but he made it clear with this witty line that if someone offers you something you need, you don't turn it down. It was okay to have pride but not to be so proud you refused stuff you needed. Here is my dad's explanation of why you don't turn things down when they are offered to you:

- You don't turn down food, because you may not get to eat tomorrow.
- You don't turn down work, because it may be gone tomorrow.
- You don't turn down clothes, because it may get cold tonight.

- And you don't turn down money, because that would just be stupid.

The best thing about Joey growing all the time was that he outgrew clothes fast. Mrs. Parker always gave me his old clothes, which was great because they were usually still in good shape. She told me once that Joey outgrew them before he had time to wear them out. The downside to this was that with all of the brothers I had, I didn't always get to wear the clothes. Just because someone gave them to me didn't mean they were mine. My favorite coat of all time was a black and gold (letter jacket type) that Joey gave to me in third grade. The coat was so cool and it was very warm. Our school mascot was the Tigers, so our colors were black and gold. I loved that coat and wore it for several years.

I am sure that Mrs. Parker helped other kids in Mansfield like she helped me and my family but I really felt as though she was my second mom. She made sure I had food, clothes, and even toys. I didn't know then, but I figured it out several years later that she fixed the Chinese gift exchange we had that year at school. I remember having a really stupid gift like a bottle of bubbles or something like that, something that no one would trade for, but then lo and behold, it was Joey's turn and he had a Monopoly board game, something really good. I think he was last to go, so after he opened the last gift, he had a choice of either keeping it and the game was over or he could trade it to someone else. I remember him walking over to me with his head down, and he picked up my bubbles and gave me the game. Of course at the time I am thinking, "How stupid is this guy," but again, a few years later I realized that his mom probably told him to do it. I know he didn't understand why just as I didn't understand why at the time, but I know he is a better person today as I know I am for the things his mom taught us with her actions back then.

Barbara Parker continued to be a major influence in my life during elementary school, junior high, and high school and even after that. Without her, I truly don't believe that I would have accomplished the things in my life that I have. I consider her one of the three or four most influential persons in my life.

While Mrs. Parker made sure I had things like food, clothing, and self-esteem, Mom and Dad Holman made sure I had things like discipline, guidance, and personal hygiene. I think between three moms, I had the potential to be somewhat of a well-rounded person. Not that my mom couldn't have done all of these things; I think she just had too much on her plate to concentrate on the little things.

There were two very influential people in my life that year and strangely enough, it wasn't Joe Holman or Joey Davis, but rather it was their mothers: Janice Holman and Barbara Parker.

The remainder of third grade went by pretty fast, almost a blur. I don't remember a whole lot about what happened at home but mainly things that happened at school or Joe's house. The one significant event during this time was the passing away of my dad's parents. Grandma Harris passed away in November of the previous year and shortly thereafter, in January, Grandpa Harris died. Daddy went to the funerals but none of us did. We never really spent much time with Grandma and Grandpa Harris. They only lived forty-five miles away in Greenville, but we still didn't visit very often. I only remember visiting their house a couple of times. I do remember them having a storm cellar that we thought was so cool. We used it as an army fort. Grandpa Harris was a farmer from the old days. He used to load all of his produce on his truck, which had special shelves built over the bed, so he could display all of the fruits and vegetables he had to sell. He would then drive all around selling produce off his truck. He would come by our house every now and then and give us some stuff.

If there has to be a silver lining on all dark clouds, then the fact that we got a second car from Grandpa Harris when he died was ours. This car was huge. It was a 1969 Pontiac Bonneville. It was white with red interior and was like brand-new. My momma was so excited because now she had her own car. Actually, having a car was nice, because a while back my dad sold his '57 Chevy and bought a pickup. Anytime we went anywhere all of us kids had to ride in the back of the truck. It didn't matter if it was 112 or 20 degrees, we rode in the back. Momma loved that car and so did we.

CHAPTER 9

The Summer Of '72

WELL, IT IS summertime again and here we are, nine kids at home with not much to do but fight with each other, bother Momma, and watch television. I'm sure there are many factors that contribute to the psyche and stability of a person as they start reaching that age when they have to decide who they are or what they are going to be in life. I think a person looks at his surroundings or his family and makes decisions to either stay on course and see where it takes them or change directions and see if they can do or be something different. That time had come for Rocky. I don't know the specifics of any conversations or fights or arguments between Rocky and Momma or Daddy, but I'm sure there had to have been some leading up to the events that summer.

The first major event during the summer of '72 was the coming of age of Rocky, the oldest of the family. I don't recall Rocky ever being in trouble even in school. He played football and was in the high school band. He must have been fifteen or sixteen years old and coming into his own manhood. There seemed to be more fighting between him and

Daddy. I don't know what about or anything else; I just know that the fights were more physical and more frequent. The last fight I remember them having started out with typical yelling and screaming but soon spilled out into the yard. I can see Rocky standing his ground like a man, refusing to back down, but the next thing I see is my dad taking Rocky to the ground, holding him down by the hair on his head. As all little brothers would do, Jerry and Andy and I were trying to help Rocky; however, I am a firm believer that no matter how big or how strong you get, there is a natural phenomenon innate in all males that prevents you from ever being able to beat up your dad. Rocky was a pretty big boy now and physically he should have been able to overpower a small, skinny old man (he was old in our eyes anyway), but he couldn't. No punches were thrown and no bones broken, but the damage was done.

The next couple of days were very sad for us. I'm not sure if Momma helped with the arrangements or if Rocky handled everything on his own. Looking back on the situation and knowing how Momma always wanted her kids to be the ones who broke the chain, I think she helped him with his decision. Rocky had decided that he was going to live with Herschel (his biological dad) in Georgia. The rest of us couldn't understand why, but I think it had something to do with becoming a man, finding your manhood, or something like that. I think Momma knew that Rocky might have a better chance of improving his life if he was in a different situation. Anyway, he left and we continued on.

That summer didn't seem much different than any other summer except that Rocky was gone. We still watched cartoons

THE SUMMER OF '72

on Saturday morning and wrestling on Saturday night and we still went fishing every other weekend or so.

I know we went fishing on many occasions in the years past, but this summer was the time I remember fishing with my dad. An outing like this was a major event for a family as big as ours. There were always one or two fights over the fishing spots and somebody always got their line too close to someone else's and everybody had to have his or her own pole or rod and reel. Daddy was the best at finding a good long stick that he could tie a line to with a sinker, hook, and bobber to make a fishing pole. This is what the younger kids used. I think the reason I remember this summer so well is because it was the first year I got a rod and reel. A rod and reel meant you were getting older because now you could cast your line across the creek and fish on bottom where the big fish are. A rod and reel usually meant that you didn't have to use a bobber because those are for babies. A rod and reel meant you could catch catfish instead of perch, Perch is what you cut up and used for bait to catch catfish. Catfish is what you took home to eat. It was a small step to manhood and I was right there.

Daddy took his fishing seriously, he didn't like a bunch of running around yelling and playing. You couldn't take your line out of the water every few minutes to see if the fish got your bait. You had to leave it in the water until Daddy said you could check it. He was the bait police. The best part of going fishing was having some RC Cola with my dad. We didn't have the one-on-one tender moments or anything like that, but I can still see my dad sitting on a log with an RC in one hand and a cigarette in the other hand, carefully watching everybody's line. He never got as excited as we did when we got a bite but he was always the first to notice a line getting a nibble. Then he would calmly call that person's name a couple of times, "John, John," and that was all you needed to hear and you knew you were getting a bite.

Like the day Momma and Daddy came home with Shelly, there are just certain days or events you remember very clearly, like what you were wearing or where you were sitting and other insignificant stuff like that. Well, the next major event in my life during that summer is another one of those days when you remember it like it was yesterday. This day was the day my mom had a serious talk with me, which at the time seemed unimportant and too grown-up for me, but I remember it well.

Andy, Jerry, Sissy, and I were in the backyard, playing "build a city." Jaimie and Trisha and Sherrill were close by, digging in the dirt. Jaimie was always digging for worms to go fishing with. Shelly was in the house with Momma. Anyway, Momma came out of the back door and told Andy to come in and watch Shelly and then she said, "John Darrel, come on and go with me to get water." (Everyone hated going to get water because you had to lift the jug; you had to stop whatever it was you were doing.) At least now we had a car, which meant we didn't have to pull the wagon down to the store to get water. The store was just over a mile down the road.

However, this was not the typical water run. On this trip Momma had a talk with me that was not like any conversation we had ever had. Keep in mind that we were not a sharing kind of family. We got in the car and headed down the road

THE SUMMER OF '72

to Dorsey's store. We had gone about halfway and Momma pulled the car over to the side of the road. Usually pulling over meant that either someone was about to get a whipping or there was something on the side of the road that someone saw that we were going to pick up. As she put the car in park, I started looking around to see if there was something I was going to get out and get. Momma looked right at me and said, "John, I want you to know that I love you very much." This is truly the first time I remember my mom ever saying that to me, "I love you." I knew something wasn't right but I just said, "I love you too." Her eyes swelled up like she was going to cry but she didn't. She continued to tell me about how she felt different since having Shelly; she said it was different in the way her body felt, not different in being a momma or anything like that. She told me about how her arms and legs had felt strange and that she just didn't feel right. She said she just wanted to tell me this so if she needed to go to the doctor or something later, I would know why and she would need me to help take care of my little sisters. She told me to keep it a secret; this was just between us. Being only nine years old, I can't remember what I thought or how I felt, but I remember the conversation. I wasn't scared or anything like that; it was more like I was special, like Momma knew I could handle this. Again, looking back, I didn't think too much about what my mom said, but it was always in the back of my head. I don't know if she had this conversation with any of my brothers or sisters or was it just between us. Our own special brief moment that was for me and no one else. We went on to the store and got the jug of water without either one of us saying anything else.

It was shortly thereafter that Momma was diagnosed with

scleroderma, which means "hardening of the skin." At the time it was a rare skin disease that very little was known about and very little could be done for. At the time, it wasn't known if the disease was hereditary or what. The symptoms were mainly of a physical nature. Basically, your skin got real tight and hard. It was not a life-threatening situation nor was it a rapidly developing disease; a person could live a long, normal, productive life with it, as long as the disease stayed on the outside of the body and didn't attack the organs.

With no insurance or money, our only neighborhood doctor was Parkland Hospital in Dallas. Parkland was the county hospital where Shelly was born. I didn't go with Mom to any of her doctor's visits at Parkland so I don't really know what was going on. I know over the next couple of months she only went to the hospital every now and then, I think mainly just for checkups and stuff. What was being done or said, I don't know. Nothing was really ever discussed or talked about in front of us, or maybe I just never noticed. Maybe Andy and Jerry were well informed since they were the oldest, but I don't know.

As if the whole Rocky moving out and Momma being diagnosed with some rare skin disease wasn't enough, we had to move again that summer. It was the same old "couldn't pay the rent" thing. There were several times that Mr. English would come to the house and Momma would send one of us to the door and tell him that neither Momma nor Daddy were home. This worked for a couple of weeks but not for long. Another silver lining though; we were paying $150 a month rent for this house, but we found another house on the other side of Webb for only $100 a month.

THE SUMMER OF '72

This house belonged to Oscar Skinner. He and his father were two of the largest cattle growers and landowners in Webb. They must have had over 2,000 acres of land in various parts of the area. This house was smaller than Mr. English's house. The workers who helped on the Skinner Dairy initially used it as their sleeping quarters. It only had two bedrooms, a living room, and a kitchen. The best thing about this house was that we could drink the water straight from the faucet. No more going to the store and hauling water. We moved during August, right before school started; I remember because it was so hot, and again there was no air-conditioning. However, there was a swamp cooler in the window of the living room. For anyone not from the south, a swamp cooler is a huge box fan that can hold water in the bottom which the fan pulls the air across and cools it down before sending it into the house. This cooling technique would reduce a room temperature of 110 degrees to about 105 degrees within a two-foot radius of the exit area of the blown air, but anything beyond the two-foot area would maintain the original 110 degrees.

The only heat for the house was also in the living room. We used butane to heat and cook with. There was a small heater about a foot wide and maybe eighteen inches tall that provided our heat. The bathroom was added on to the back of the house. It consisted of a sink, a toilet, a hot water heater, and a stall with a pipe running up the wall with a showerhead on it. No bathtub. Daddy put a smaller heater in the bathroom after we moved in, but he was the only one allowed to turn it on, not because it was complicated, but Momma was the only one worthy of having heat while she went to the bathroom.

The bedroom that faced the north was an addition and had a

wood floor and wood walls. This was Momma and Daddy's room. Except for the winter, Trisha and Shelly and sometimes Jaimie slept in there too; this room was uninhabitable during the winter. It would get so cold in there that you literally didn't need a freezer or refrigerator. The rest of us slept in the other bedroom. The room was big enough for two beds and a dresser. We didn't really worry about whose drawer was whose; basically all clothing in the house belonged to whoever could wear it at the time.

The living room, the kitchen, and the other bedroom had concrete floors and plaster walls. During the winter most everyone slept in the living room. We would put plastic and blankets over the doorways into the bedrooms to keep out the cold and keep in the heat. If you were brave enough or just wanted a big bed to yourself, you could put on three or four sets of clothes, load up a couple of blankets, and sleep in the kids' bedroom. I think Andy and Jerry did this quite often. The ceiling was plaster but the roof was sheets of tin. Being out in the country and living in a time when people didn't always lock their cars or houses, this house didn't even have locks on the doors or window. Daddy put a latch and a hook on the outside of the front door so he could put a padlock on it when we all went somewhere. I don't really remember the door getting locked very often because he was the only one with a key. Generally the house was open.

As we got settled in the new house, we met a man named Mr. Elvis Lamb. He owned quite a bit of land across the street and down the road from our house. He was a part-time farmer who also had a day job in Grand Prairie. I think his daddy was a full-time farmer and used to live in the old house that Mr.

Lamb now used for storage and stuff. Nobody had lived in it for the past thirty years or so. Mr. Lamb would come out to his farmhouse almost every night and always every weekend to tend to his cows and fields. He grew mainly hay for feed and sometimes he would grow some corn to sell.

Andy, Jerry, and I did a lot of work for Mr. Lamb. Usually it was hay hauling but sometimes we would help him put up some fencing or repair a barn or something else like that. Mr. Lamb was a slow-talking farmer who knew almost everything about everything. He would talk politics, religion, farming, parenting, and even science. He had a remedy for anything that ailed you. He was a good friend to us and really helped our family out. Jerry was his favorite because he would spend hours down there with Mr. Lamb and listen to him talk. Mr. Lamb loved to talk and talk and talk.

We got to be good friends with Mr. Lamb. The three of us boys hauled a lot of hay and did a lot of work for him over the next seven or eight years. Mr. Lamb was a very smart man. He was a teacher of life and a good role model for us. It was always best to get paid by the hour when you worked for him though, because once he started telling you a story or something, he would talk forever. He was a dictionary farmer. Meaning if you looked up the word "farmer" in the dictionary, all it would say is "refer to Mr. Lamb." He always wore jeans and a long-sleeved button-down shirt, usually a jean shirt or some type of Dickie brand shirt. I never saw him without a high-rise cap and a chaw of tobacco. He chewed plug tobacco. He was a hardworking man too. He worked his day job every day and then farmed in the evenings and weekends. Usually from sunup to sundown and later on the weekends.

There was a small section of land right next to our house that Mr. Skinner said we could use for a garden, so Mr. Lamb brought his big tractor and plowed it up for us. We started out trying to plow it with just hand tools but it was too big. We planted a lot of different things over the years ranging from okra to watermelons. We raised tomatoes, squash, cucumbers, cantaloupe, and even some onions. We never got a lot of anything from the garden and what we got wasn't that great, because we didn't irrigate, but we got enough to eat. The only thing we kids got tired of was okra. I think okra would grow in a parking lot with no water and in 110-degree heat.

In the back corner, we built a pretty big chicken house with a small fenced-in area. We didn't eat the chickens so much as we raised them for eggs. At different times, we would have a couple of ducks, maybe a rabbit or two or twenty, and we had a couple of pigs for a while. One of the funniest things to watch is when a chicken gets stuck in the pig pen and the pig tears the chicken to pieces. We thought it was funny but of course Daddy didn't.

We had a small porch off the back door that led to the bathroom and to the outside. My momma said she must have been living right for a while, because Daddy rigged a water line to that back porch and put in a washing machine. No more having to go to the Laundromat. It was so great to be able to wash clothes whenever you needed to, rather than waiting till Saturday. Saturday was usually the day Daddy got paid and we would all, or almost all, load up and go to the Laundromat and wash clothes. Even though it was a big pain in the butt, I remember it being a fun day. We got to go to town and spend

THE SUMMER OF '72

several hours somewhere other than home. The Laundromat was a pretty cool place.

When you don't have a lot of toys around the house, you find ways to make games and have fun with anything new. We used to push each other in the laundry baskets and have races around the washing machines. The most exciting thing about the Laundromat was the thrill of finding money. I remember Momma making us lie on the floor looking under every machine. We would use a clothes hanger to sweep under each machine, dragging out dirt, lint, and whatever else was under there, but we almost always found some loose change. Anyway, we didn't have to go to the Laundromat anymore. The downside to having a washing machine is not having a dryer. We would hang the clothes outside on the fence to dry. The bad thing about this was that the fence was a barb-wire fence. If you were not careful taking the clothes off, you would rip them. I think every piece of clothing, towel, and sheet in our house had rips.

Actually the water was not the best thing about this house. The fact that the bus stopped right in front of our house was the best. At our previous house, we had to walk to the bus stop, which was in town at Dorsey's store, just over a mile or so.

That year for Christmas we got a bike. It was an old used bike that Pawpaw picked up on his trash route. In fact, we got it a couple of days after Christmas. I am guessing that someone got a new one and threw away the old one, but we thought it was great. With five or six kids all at different levels of bike-riding expertise, that bike was put through hell. Jerry was the daredevil. He would build ramps out of rocks and pieces of wood so he could jump over stuff. We would even lie side by side and see how many of us he could jump over. Not good for the ones at the end, but you had to pay your dues if you wanted to ride next.

The best game we came up with was "he who stops it gets to ride it." Basically someone would ride back and forth down the street and the others would try to stop it or knock him or her off of it. The winner got to ride next. You could throw things into the spokes (like a stick or broom handle), you could throw yourself in front of the bike to stop it, or you could jump in and grab the handlebars and try to take it from the rider. Basically anything was good. Lots of scrapes, bumps, cuts, and such, but it was fun. Later that spring, Mr. Skinner gave us another bike; I think it was one that his son Howard outgrew. Now with two bikes the games got better. We had several variations of jousting and demolition derby.

CHAPTER **10**

The Fall Of '72

SHELLY IS A year old now and probably walking. Trisha is just over three years old, Jaimie is five, Sherrill is six and starting first grade, Sissy is seven and going to second grade, and here I am, nine years old and headed into the fourth grade. Rocky and Robert are still living with Herschel, and I believe Robert is in the fourth grade as well because he was held back in second grade. Jerry is twelve and going into the fifth grade. Jerry was held back as well in either first or second grade, I'm not sure which. That is why he is not in the sixth grade this year. Andy is big time; he is fourteen and in the eighth grade. We haven't heard from Rocky or anything but I'm sure he's doing okay.

Daddy is now working for Trans Tex Supply Company in Arlington. Trans Tex sells and delivers plastic pipes, fire hydrants, and other water and sewage pipe accessories. There are several upsides to this job for Daddy; they have a retirement plan and he seems to really like driving a truck. I think he started out on a small truck making local deliveries, but soon moved up to the forty-foot bed truck and makes long hauls. Every now and then he is gone overnight but not very often. Usually if the delivery is in San Antonio or somewhere like that, he will just bring the truck home with him and leave out at three or four in the morning and still be back home that night. He seems very happy.

Another upside to Trans Tex was the opportunity for Daddy to make some extra money mowing a field next to their storage area. Daddy took the job, but it ended up being me, Jerry, and Daddy. At the time of the actual work I think the field must have been about fifty acres. We had to mow it with a barely working push mower and a couple of idiot sticks (sometimes referred to as weed whackers or yo-yos). An idiot stick was a long-handled tool with a two-sided blade on the end. A person would swing the tool back and forth, cutting down very tall grass. The name came from the fact that if you are mowing something with this tool, then you must be an idiot. Anyway, we were paid $25 for mowing this monstrosity of a field. As I drive by that field today, I see that it is really just a tad bit less than a half-acre. But back then it was at least fifty acres.

Another side job that my dad took was building meter boxes. This job was a little bit more fun for us kids. Building meter boxes consisted of a round tin thing ranging from twenty to twenty-eight inches tall and about eighteen inches in diameter. You would place a cast-iron ring on top of the round tin thing and lift it up on a steel sawhorse. The cast-iron ring had four small holes in it, to which you would insert a steel rivet from the inside of the round tin thing. Next you had to

THE FALL OF '72

use a special hammer (regular hammer head on one side and an adapted ball peen hammer with a hole in the end on the other side) to punch the rivet up through the round tin thing, and then flatten it over so it secured the cast-iron ring onto the round tin thing. This job was something we did on the weekends or my dad would stay and do it after work during the week.

Fourth grade was a little different than third but nothing major. Joe Holman was still my best friend, Joey still brought me snacks and clothes and stuff, and we were still known as the Conn kids. Everyone knew we were poor. Everyone except Mrs. Johnson. She was a new teacher and apparently didn't get the memo. The one that read, "Don't mess with Marilyn Harris or her kids."

Mrs. Johnson called me up to her desk one day during class and asked me if my mother had seen the way I was dressed that day. I had no idea what she was talking about but of course I saw Momma that morning. Mrs. Johnson proceeded to write out a note for me to give to my mom. I don't know about other children, but all of us sure got a kick out of seeing Momma mad at somebody other than us. When Momma was reading the note at home, she was getting mad. Of course we encouraged the situation the best we could, with comments like, "Momma, you oughta go beat her up," and "She can't tell you what to do; you ain't even in her class" and stuff like that. The note explained to Mrs. Harris that she should take more interest and care in the way her children were dressed for school. My hands were dirty and the clothes I was wearing were not presentable for school. Well, the next day when most kids would have been embarrassed if their mom came into the classroom to talk to the teacher, I stood proud and happy as my momma let her have it. By the way, Mrs. Johnson was also the first black teacher I ever had. But believe me, that made no difference to Momma. It wouldn't have mattered if Mrs. Johnson was white, Indian, Chinese, whatever. I can't remember her exact words that morning but it was something to the effect of: "What my kids wear to school has nothing to do with you or with them learning. You are here to teach them, not to dress them. If you don't like what my son is wearing, then you can take your black ass to the store and buy him something else. Otherwise, don't be sending home any more notes that don't have something to do with his grades or acting up in class." And she left.

The next day, I thought Mrs. Johnson had gone plumb crazy. She handed me another note to give to my mom. I took the note home and gave it to Momma. She began reading it, but only to herself, not out loud, as all of us stood around waiting for her to go off. But she never did. She told Andy to get her a pencil. She wrote something back on the note and said, "John, give this to Mrs. Johnson tomorrow." Mrs. Johnson's note was in an envelope when I brought it home, but Momma's wasn't. We took the note into the kitchen and Andy read it. As he read it to himself, he pushed me and said, "You punk, you get some new clothes." The note Mrs. Johnson wrote to my mom was an apology note and was asking permission to take me after school to purchase a few things. Of course Momma wrote back, that would be fine with her.

The next day after school, Mrs. Johnson took me to Gibson's and bought me three pairs of pants, three shirts, and a pair of shoes. I was in heaven. The best thing about it was that my pants didn't fit anyone else. When you are smaller than your older brothers, you can always wear their clothes; you just tighten up the belt or wear a big shirt. But, when you have clothes that fit you just right, they are too small for the older brothers. I cannot remember ever having a brand-new pair of shoes. Shoes that were never worn by an older brother or Joey Davis or anyone else. Brand-new. This was great. Mrs. Johnson became one of my favorite teachers fast.

Everything seemed to be going okay. Daddy liked his new job; he had extra work to make money; we were paying less rent for the house; another child was in school, which meant less food needed at home; Shelly was old enough to eat table food with the rest of us, no more special milk or anything like that. Things appeared to be pretty good. At least we thought.

Even though it had only been a couple of months since my mom was diagnosed with scleroderma, things seemed to be moving a little quicker than what was originally explained. Momma wasn't going to Parkland Hospital anymore. I don't know if the doctors decided she could be treated better or if it was closer, but now she went to John Peter Smith in Ft. Worth. JPS is the county hospital for Tarrant County.

Momma's skin was really starting to tighten up on her arms and legs. You couldn't tell so much by looking from a distance but if you got close enough to feel them, you could tell. It was like they were made of leather. They were kind of shiny and smooth, but not real hard. She still had full movement and I don't remember her being in pain or anything like that.

For about two months, I guess up until November or December,

Momma would go to JPS twice a week for some type of therapy. They would massage her arms and legs with lotion and stuff. She would soak in a whirlpool or hot bath and they would send some lotion home with her to apply three or four times a day. During this period, I stayed home from school at least once a week and either went with Momma to JPS to watch the younger kids or stayed at home with them while she went. Nothing really changed during these first couple of months, but then in December of that year, the first major change took place.

One day, Momma noticed a sore on the back of her hand and within a couple of days the sore covered almost the whole back of her hand. The doctors said something to the effect that it was just a natural progression of her skin tightening up and it should be okay. I'm not sure what order but within the next five or six weeks or so, the sore got bigger and now both of her feet and her other hand had the same big sores. It was kind of strange in that they weren't regular sores. They didn't bleed or anything; they just made a type of crater in her hands and feet. They would scab over and develop pus, but they never got smaller. I know so much about them because I would doctor them for her. I had to clean them and reapply a salve and wrap them with gauze bandages. The skin around the sores would soon start becoming dry and flaky. I would rub lotion on her hands and feet every morning before school and then a couple of times in the evening and always right before she went to bed. Her arms and legs were starting to bruise and hurt real bad with just the slightest bump or hit. Her skin would break open and crack.

So that she wouldn't have to sleep in a bed with two or three

THE FALL OF '72

kids, Daddy bought a twin bed and set it up in the living room for her. He thought the cold weather in their bedroom might be drying her skin out more as well.

One night while all of us kids were lying on the floor watching TV, Daddy was sitting in his chair, and Momma was lying in her bed, she called me over and asked me to put lotion on her legs. As a nine- or ten-year-old should do, I huffed, slapped the floor, got up, stomped my way over to her bed with my head hung down, and in sheer pain began to apply the lotion. I hate myself sometimes now for some of the things I thought back then when I had to scratch my mom's legs or put lotion on her back or whatever. Anyway, as I sat on the end of her bed rubbing lotion on her legs, she looked down at me and mouthed, "I love you," the second time in just over a year that I can remember. I wanted to cry, I didn't, but went to the bathroom before anybody saw me. After I got myself together I came back and rubbed lotion on my mom's legs, arms, and back for over an hour. That night I slept on the floor next to her bed for the first time. The next morning, Momma woke me up earlier than anyone else. She told me to sit by her and she put her arms around me and she just held me. She didn't say anything, she just held me. We sat there for probably ten minutes. Neither of us saying a word.

I know it took several months, but it seemed like overnight. It was as if we woke up one morning and Momma was officially sick. Starting from her feet, the sores would clear up to almost gone, and then they would come back just a little while later. Her lower legs had very little substance and you could see each bone, as skin appeared to have been shrinking around them. It can best be described as a piece of plastic wrap being heat shrunk around something. Her upper legs were not as bad. They still had some elasticity to them but not much. At this time she still had pretty good movement in her knees but it was getting worse. The skin was tightening up so much it was restricting her movement. The same was true for her arms. Her fingers were beginning to draw in at each knuckle. She was losing movement in her wrist and her elbows. The lower part of her arms was much like her legs. The skin was beginning to tighten up and appeared to be like a petrified piece of wood. In fact, the *Ft. Worth Star-Telegram* newspaper did a story on her and the title was "Mother of Nine Turns to Wood." Sounds like a story from the *National Enquirer*. The upper part of her arms, like her thighs, still had some elasticity. The doctors continued her physical therapy, trying to maintain what motion she still had.

The restricted motion had not taken her ability to move. She walked a little slower but still managed to get around. Her visits to JPS continued every Monday, Wednesday, and Friday now. I hated that place. We would sit and wait for hours. Everybody knew us by now and it was just a part of our life. I think I missed school at least once or twice a week during the fourth grade. It didn't really matter though. I still made good grades. Mrs. Johnson always let me make up any work that I had missed and there were never any questions about me missing school.

Momma still got around okay at home. She would spend her days taking care of Shelly, Trisha, and Jaimie. She would feed the chickens, gather eggs, and watch her stories. "Stories" was another way of saying soap operas. Her favorite was *Days*

THE FALL OF '72

of Our Lives, followed by *All My Children* and *As the World Turns*. These were the top daytime dramas on at the time.

I am sure that when she heard that bus come around the corner at 4:00, the thought of five more kids coming home chased away all the quiet time she had enjoyed all day. Our evenings after school were spent pretty much outside. I don't remember having much homework or homework time in the evenings. We would generally play outside for a while, usually until Daddy got home, and then we knew it was time to eat. We never ate until Daddy got home. I don't know why, or who made that rule; it is just the way it was. If by some chance Daddy got home at 5:30, then we ate at 5:30, but if he didn't get home until 6:45, then we didn't eat until 6:45. Dinner would be ready, sitting on the stove, and as soon as the first one of us kids saw Daddy's truck, he/she would yell out, "Daddy's home." Everyone would run in the house and start serving plates. We always had a pitcher of tea to go with dinner as well. I don't know that we ever had enough glasses for everyone to have a glass or cup for their tea, so several of us usually drank out of a tin can that was left from a can of vegetables.

After dinner was usually television time. This is when we would watch for the hundredth time the reruns of *I Love Lucy*, *Gilligan's Island*, and *The Dick Van Dyke Show* and of course, *Gunsmoke*. Every now and then if some of us were outside, Andy would sneak in some *Star Trek*. He was the only one in the family who liked that show, so he rarely got to watch it.

Dinner was pretty constant at our house. We almost always had a big pot of pinto beans, sometimes navy beans, sometimes black-eyed peas, but usually it was pinto beans or red beans as my granny called them. Besides beans, we would have some type of vegetable, depending on what we had grown in the garden. The other staple was potatoes, fried potatoes. I would estimate that 80 percent of the supper meals at our house were beans and taters. The other two things that were at every meal was a loaf of bread and tea. A loaf of day-old bread was pretty cheap and I think it was a good filler.

The special days at our house were when Daddy got paid and Mommy would go to his work during the day and get his check. Then she would either get a bucket of Kentucky Fried Chicken or she would stop at the store and get sandwich meat. Not just bologna, but she would get either pickle loaf or ham. Every now and then, Momma would make meatloaf, and that was truly a special day. Now I must say here that I made that same meatloaf (many years later) for my wife, and she said that she didn't know if she was eating breakfast or dinner, because there was so much oatmeal in the meatloaf. I never really thought about why my momma put a whole box of oatmeal in with one pound of hamburger meat to make meatloaf, but then I realized that is how you feed nine or ten people with just a pound or so of hamburger. Anyway, I loved my momma's meatloaf, as did everyone else in the family.

With all of Momma's brothers and sisters living within driving distance to us, it seems as though there was always somebody at our house, especially on the weekend. With just beans and taters as the mainstay for meals, everyone was welcome to stay and eat. Momma never turned anyone away, unless there was meat involved. One Saturday afternoon, several of us had gone to town for something and Momma stopped and got a

THE FALL OF '72

big bucket of Kentucky Fried Chicken. When we drove into the driveway, we saw Uncle Melvin's car. This meant there were six more people to feed. Momma stuck that bucket under the front seat and told us to keep our mouths shut. She was not going to feed that bunch our chicken. After several hours and a small meal of beans and fried squash, Melvin and his family left. Momma yelled at me to go get the chicken so we could eat. We didn't even heat it up; we all just sat there and each ate one piece of cold chicken.

Momma usually had the beans pretty much ready by the time we got home from school since they had to be cooked for a couple of hours. We would peel potatoes or cut up and bread some okra or squash, but for the most part dinner was pretty simple. As for breakfast, I honestly don't remember eating much more than a piece of toast or maybe some oatmeal every now and then or if one of the older kids would cook them, we would have some scrambled eggs. When we got up in the morning, we simply got dressed and waited for the bus to get there, watching Slam Bang Theater, which featured *The Three Stooges* and various cartoons. Since we were so far out, the bus usually got to our house about 7:20, and school started at 8:10 back then. Lunch was easy during the school year. Remember, we all got free lunches.

The holidays were never very memorable. We didn't decorate the house very much, there weren't a lot of family get-togethers, and there for sure weren't a lot of presents at Christmastime, but this year was a little different. A few days before Christmas someone knocked on the door late in the evening. We were all shocked; we never had people visit who knocked on the door. My aunts and uncles just walked in, no knocking. Well, we all jumped up to see who it was. Daddy was yelling for us all to move back and when he opened the door, it was a large group of people from some church. They all started coming in singing Christmas songs and carrying lots of presents. They stayed for ten or fifteen minutes, but when they left, they left all of the presents. There were at least three for each of us. Momma wouldn't let us open them until Christmas, but I tell you it was the best Christmas ever. I remember exactly what I got that year. I got a Yahtzee game, a pair of jeans, and a Mansfield Tigers sweatshirt that fit me perfectly and it was brand-new. I loved that sweatshirt and wore it for several years, even when it didn't fit so well.

CHAPTER **11**

Spring Of '73

AS BEST AS I can recall, the physical aspects of Momma's disease seemed to have slowed down, but that may have been more of us just getting used to them. She was still moving around quite well and the sores didn't seem to be getting any worse. They were still only on the tops of her feet and hands. The most dramatic physical change that we could see was her hair. Momma was slowly losing her hair. Nothing major but when one of my siblings or I brushed her hair, we could see more falling out. The only other significant thing was her weight. Momma was beginning to get skinny. She was a fairly stout woman who weighed in at around 150 pounds in her prime. She didn't seem to eat as much as she used to, and whether this was related to the medications she was taking or the fact that she wasn't nearly as active as she used to be, I don't know. She still liked to have a Dr. Pepper and a bag of Frito's every now and then, but not much else.

I have no idea what the mental toll is on a person once they have been diagnosed with a disease that is probably going to be with them the rest of their life, one that is so rare that there are no cures, no treatments, and only a handful of things that doctors can do to help ease the pain and physical stress that your body will be going through. But I do know that Momma never let it show what it was doing to her mentally. I don't know how I would handle knowing that I could have this disease for the next forty or fifty years. I cannot recall my momma going to church, and I can honestly say that she did not have the "it is God's will" mentality about things, but at the same time, I never heard the "why me?" thing either. Momma was a lot like Daddy in the sense that she never blamed other people, God, or anything else for things that happened. You have what you have, you are what you are, and the only thing you can do is to make the best with what you have today, and try to make it better tomorrow. While she never asked for pity or sympathy, there were some frustrations.

Momma was a very independent woman and I think the fact that she had to rely on others to help her do things made her mad. She didn't want to be a burden to the rest of us and it was frustrating that sometimes there was nothing else she could do. The girls in our family were as tough or even a little tougher than the boys. They played just as rough, they fought just as hard, and they were treated the same. Momma never babied the girls but sometimes the feminine side would shine through. There were times when one of the girls would want her hair in braids or ponytails and of course Momma would oblige.

One night the reality of Momma's limitations and her lack of dexterity became obvious to me. Sherrill had asked Momma to put her hair in a ponytail. After what seemed like a long time, Momma called me to come over and shoo this fly away from her. We were all lying around on the floor watching television and of course I was mad that I had to stop watching and go over to Momma's bed to be on fly patrol. When I didn't see a fly around her, I was even more mad, but with a head nod and a mother's own eye movement, I realized Momma really just wanted me to pull Sherrill's hair back and put the barrettes in without Sherrill knowing that it wasn't Momma doing it. Momma's hands were involved enough now that she couldn't hold Sherrill's hair with one hand and manipulate the barrette with the other. It only took a couple of minutes but I realized that Momma was sad that she couldn't even do the little things a momma wants to do for her kids and for herself.

As the scleroderma set in, Momma's arms and legs were most affected. She started using crutches to get around quite a bit but they made her arms sore, so it wasn't long before she used the wheelchair more and more around the house. The wheelchair was great once she was in it but she had a really hard time transferring over from her bed, so one of us had to help her. At first we would just pull her to a standing position, she would turn herself while holding on to us, and then someone else would push the chair up to her. This was okay but I think it made her nervous, so my dad, being the smart man he is, made her a sliding board thing. Basically it was a two-inch by two-inch board about three feet long that was sanded down real well so it was slick or slippery. Now when Momma wanted to get in her chair, one of us would get the wheelchair and she could hold on to us and slide herself into the chair. The only problem with the board was that it was so heavy she couldn't do it by herself. She still used the crutches to go outside or to smack one of us with if we weren't doing what she told us to do, but she mainly used the wheelchair.

CHAPTER **12**

Fall Of '73

AS THE SUMMER of '73 rolled into the fall, school was getting close and now Momma would only have two kids at home during the day. Shelly was two, Trisha was four, and Jamie was six and starting first grade. Sherrill was seven, moving into second; Sissy was eight and going into third; I was ten years old and going into fifth; Jerry was thirteen and going into seventh; and Andy was fifteen and in high school.

As people in general will do, we (the kids) learned how to adapt to and make the best out of each situation. One day, Jerry and I were walking home from town, no hurry, no agenda, just taking our time and out of the blue, we saw an old beat-up basketball in the ditch. It was still inflated, still bounced, and it still worked. So we had fun with it all the way home.

We played all kinds of games with it, dodge ball, kick ball, tag ball, everything except basketball. We didn't have a hoop. But necessity breeds creativity. We took an old piece of plywood and a bicycle rim. Jerry took all of the spokes out of the

FALL OF '73

old tire wheel and we nailed it to the plywood, then nailed the plywood to a telephone pole that was set next to the road. Boom, instant basketball goal. We played on that goal for several years, and it was great.

Daddy was still driving the truck and working hard on the weekends. He always seemed to find a way for either him or some of us boys to make some extra money or at least some work that we could do to reduce the amount of rent we had to pay that month. Mr. Skinner, our landlord, took care of a lot of cows and pastures. There always seemed to be fences that needed to be fixed or something that needed to be done.

During one Christmas break, which was about two weeks back then, Jerry, Andy, and I had the privilege of helping Mr. Skinner clear up a section of land that he was using to graze his cows. The job entailed quite a bit of manual labor. My dad would drop us off at the pasture on his way to work in the morning, around six, and we would wait for the sun to come up so we could get to work. We used grubbing hoes, which is a tool that has a long wooden handle with an iron piece attached to one end. The iron piece was a combination hoe and pick. One side had a flat blade type of tool and the other side was a pointed pick, which was used to break up hard ground or to bust up rocks and stuff, and the flat blade side was used to dig up something or to hoe an area for planting. We used the hoe side to dig up small to medium mesquite bushes from this twenty-acre pasture. We would then pile the bushes up and periodically throughout the day Mr. Skinner would come around with his pickup and we would load up the bushes to be taken away and burned. We would work until Daddy picked us up on his way home from work, which was usually around 6:00 or 6:30. We did this for ten days of our Christmas vacation. We didn't get paid for it; Mr. Skinner took some money off the rent for that month. I don't remember any one of us complaining about it either; it was just us doing our part.

Not all of the work we did for Mr. Skinner and others around Webb was to relieve some type of debt. We got paid for hauling hay, feeding cows, and doing other odd jobs, and that money, or at least most of it, was ours to keep. Almost every weekend we had "family time," sort of. We would all load up in the back of Daddy's truck with lots of trash bags and go can hunting. Recycling was virtually nonexistent during my youth, but one thing that was recycled was aluminum cans. Mainly beer cans and soft drink cans. Most food was sold in metal cans, but not beer and soft drinks. As with a lot of things, littering on the country roads was not a big deal back in the day. There were no fines for it; people just threw stuff out the window, no big deal.

Daddy would drive to certain areas of Mansfield and Arlington that were heavily traveled, and we would go to work. We would all hop out of the truck with three or four on each side of the road and we starting hunting cans. The younger kids did most of the hunting and the older, bigger boys did the stomping and carrying. As the little kids found cans, they would throw them up on the road and the boys would stomp them flat. This would save room in the bags so you could get more in each. The going rate at the time was ten to fifteen cents per pound. There were several places around town where you would take your cans, and they would weigh them and pay you your money. These outings usually lasted four or five hours, depending how successful the hunt was going. Every now and then we would hit the jackpot and find a bunch of soda bottles. During this time, when you purchased a soft drink in a bottle, you had to pay a deposit of five cents. When you brought the bottle back to any convenience store or grocery store, you would get paid five cents for each bottle, and it was a lot better to find a bunch of bottles than an equal number of cans. We did this for many years, especially as the price of aluminum cans kept going up. Of course there were little tricks to help your cans weigh more, like filling several of them with dirt and putting them in the bottom of the bag, but if you got caught, the man wouldn't take your cans and you had to find another place to sell them.

These were just a few things we all did to support the family. It was never a question about going or not; we all went, we all helped, and that was just the way it was, "family time."

Even though it had only been a couple of years since Momma was first diagnosed with scleroderma, it seemed as though it had been my whole life. There were daily lotion applications on her legs, arms, and back. I spent several hours a week doctoring her feet and hands, by changing the gauze pads and applying new salve. If the scabs were bothering her, I used my dad's toenail clippers to try to remove some of the bigger ones. Momma was in constant pain by then, but as with all things, I think a person gets used to it or accepts the situation as a part of life. She was taking a pain medication called Tylenol 3, which from my understanding was a pretty potent pain reliever for the time. She would take them two or three at a time several times a day. My nights of sleeping on the floor next to her bed had now become the norm, not the exception, as she needed her pain pills more often during the night and would need to go to the bathroom more often.

At ten or eleven years old, it never occurred to me how my mom must have felt having to have her children help her get onto the toilet, or empty her bed pan, or give her a sponge bath while she lay in bed. The things I did were just things that Momma needed to have done and there was never an issue with dignity or privacy. The fact that it seems as though Momma picked me more than the others was probably because Momma wanted to keep the embarrassment of the rest of the kids to a minimum. By picking me, what I mean is that Momma called on me to do a lot more for her in certain areas of her care than others. After a while I was very perceptive at reading her tone of voice or the language she used when she called one of us. I knew by the way she called my name that she needed an itch scratched or she needed to be turned or maybe she needed her bed pan quickly, so I was quick to respond without anyone else in the family really noticing what was going on. I am not saying that I was more mature than anyone else, but I think maybe I had a better understanding of what was going on.

With a family as big and as lacking financially as we were, we never had many family outings for dinner or vacations or things of that nature, but with the progression the scleroderma, it was even more difficult for Momma to get around, so even things like trips to the grocery store were getting fewer and farther between. I do remember a couple of adventures during that year that were very interesting.

Momma decided one Saturday that we were all going to the

drive-in to see a movie. Drive-in theaters were fairly cheap back then, but when you have eight kids and two adults, nothing is really cheap. But nonetheless, we were going to the movie. I recall Momma and Daddy talking on the way about how much money they had and the best way to get us all in the movie. Well, here is how you get that many people into a movie and only pay for the two adults. We stopped just outside of the entrance and Daddy opened the trunk and all of us older kids got inside, leaving only Jaimie, Trisha, and Shelly in the backseat. Kids under six got in free. So there you go.

CHAPTER **13**

The Winter Of '74

THE WINTER WAS coming and the cold weather was always worse for Momma. I think the cold made her skin even drier and hard, which made the pain worse. In November, Momma was in so much pain that Daddy took her to John Peter Smith hospital when he got home that night and they admitted her for observation. This was her first overnight stay that I can remember. I don't recall what went on during that hospital stay; we all assumed that they were watching her to see what was going on. She was only there for about three days. When Momma came home she assured us that it was nothing and those doctors didn't know what they were doing anyway.

Even with everything happening to her, Momma always had a pretty good sense of humor or at least a good tolerance of things. She did her share of yelling at us or throwing things at us if need be, but she was still very outgoing and upbeat about most things. She had a very matter-of-fact attitude about her. For example, we all came home from school one day, one by one filing out of the bus and everybody making a run for the front door. We stood around the living room; the television was on, Shelly and Trisha were lying on a blanket asleep, but Momma wasn't there. She must be in the bathroom, we decided. So several of us ran back there, but no mom. Like a search party, we all hit the back door and scattered, looking around. I think Andy was the first to start laughing, but within a few seconds we were all rolling on the ground. Momma was in the chicken yard (a fenced-in area about twelve by twelve feet around the chicken house, with only one gate in or out) and was standing in the corner, leaning on one crutch and the fence, waving her other crutch at Matilda. Matilda was a goose, a very mean goose that our granny had given to us. Matilda would chase us kids around the yard, nipping at our heels or the back of our legs. Nothing very serious but occasionally she could hurt you. Anyway, while Momma was gathering eggs, Matilda apparently decided she wanted to play. Momma said that damn goose wouldn't let her out of the chicken yard. She kept flapping her wings, honking and biting at Momma's feet. Momma had been stuck out there for almost an hour and she was mad, really mad. She was so mad that we had goose for dinner that night. When Daddy got home, Momma made him hold that goose down and she personally chopped her head off. We were kind of sad about Matilda being gone, but then again, we had a great dinner that night. Momma was fine with most things and usually would roll with the punches, but don't make her mad. Matilda found out the hard way.

With Momma getting less and less mobile, it seems as though there were always people at our house on the weekends instead of us going to their house. It may also have been that my aunts and uncles really didn't want all of us coming to their house. My aunt Linda, as you may remember, was my mom's younger sister. Her husband Charles and their two kids, Charles Joe and little Sissy, were our most frequent guests. Of course there was Melvin and Shirley and their four girls always showing up in time to eat. As little as we had, Momma and Daddy never seemed to mind it when family came over.

The best part about my aunts and uncles coming over was when the grown-ups played poker. The round table we got for Christmas several years earlier with the Formica top was perfect for six to eight people to sit around and play cards. They didn't always play poker; sometimes they played dominoes or spades, but to me poker was the best. There was money involved in poker. I don't know that I ever saw more than five or six dollar bills on the table at one time, but there was always lot of silver: nickels, dimes and quarters. When my uncle Melvin was playing there would be lots of pennies. I mean four or five dollars' worth of pennies, but nobody ever complained. The general rule when the grown-ups were playing poker was that the kids had to be outside or in any other room of the house, but not the kitchen. That rule didn't apply to me. I think this was the payback from my mom for all the stuff I did for her. Momma's hands and fingers had been affected by the scleroderma to the point she couldn't bend her fingers in or straighten them out more than halfway, making it hard for her to hold the cards or pick up the money while they played. So I got to sit next to her and hold her cards and make her bets for her. I learned how to play poker, spades, canasta, and forty-two dominoes at the age of ten or eleven. Sometimes I would want to go out and play with the other kids if they were playing football, but for the most part I liked holding my mom's cards.

THE WINTER OF '74

They would play cards for several hours or until everybody lost their money. Melvin was always the big loser. He never seemed to win anything. Everyone else seemed to rotate winnings. Momma would win this week but Aunt Linda would win next time, and then Charles and Daddy would both come out good on the next. But never Melvin. He was the Eeyore of our family. Everything was doom and gloom. But all in all everyone would have a good time. There was never enough money on the table to make the night a life-changing event; just enough to have some jingle in your pocket and bragging rights until next time.

After the poker game we all managed to find a seat somewhere in the living room, the grown-ups on the couch or in a chair and all thirteen or fourteen kids sitting or lying on the floor. Saturday night always ended the same way for us, whether we had company or not; we always watched the country and western variety shows and the old western shows. The staples were shows like *Bonanza*, *Rawhide*, and *The Rifleman*. The variety shows included *Hee Haw*, *The Porter Wagoner Show* and the *Grand Ole Opry*. However, the night was not over until *Saturday Night Wrestling*. Sometimes everyone would spend the night and we would all spend Sunday either working on someone's car or going to the flea market or the grown-ups would simply sit around talking while all of us played or fought amongst ourselves. It was a simple life, but it was good.

As time went on and the physical aspects of the scleroderma got worse, Momma adapted. For example, when she couldn't get her hands close enough to her mouth to take her pills, she got good at leaning her head back, raising her arm about six inches above her mouth, and dropping the pill in. She could still hold a cup and drink from a straw. This worked pretty well for a while. I think she went through all of this to maintain some semblance of independence. Every now and then when she missed with a pill, she would still have to call one of us to pick it up for her but then she would try again. Later on though, her medicine consumption increased from several times a day to many times a day, so she accepted the fact that it was easier just to have me feed her the pills and hold the glass for her. It really wasn't an issue with us as much as it was admitting one more defeat for her.

One thing that Momma accepted a little easier than some of the other things was the loss of her hair. At first, she was very self-conscious about it. She had a wig that my aunt Linda had gotten for her. It was the same color as her own hair but it was short. She wore it almost all the time. Even just around the house. It seemed so commonplace to us to hear Momma say, "Someone hand me my hair," but for people outside the circle that may have sounded a bit strange. But as with other conditions and problems that come with being sick, the more you get accustomed to things, the less important they become. After a few months of having the wig, Momma never really wore it around the house unless we had company. She still wore it when she went to the store or the hospital but it definitely was not a top priority anymore. She did discover another use for it, however.

One day we were going to one of her regularly scheduled doctors' appointments at JPS. Keep in mind that even with declining mobility in her arms, legs, hands, and feet, Momma still drove. She was a good driver, she only had one accident

THE WINTER OF '74

that I can remember, but sometimes if her fingers got tangled up in the steering wheel or if they slipped off the steering wheel, well, she might venture over into someone else's lane a little, which she did on this particular day. As she regained control and moved her car back into her lane, the guy she almost ran over pulled up beside us and used his middle finger to show his displeasure with Momma's driving abilities. Well, as all friendly people should do, Momma tried to give him a reciprocal greeting, but as she held her hand up to give him the finger, she gave five slightly bent and skinny fingers. I didn't see the man's response but I heard Momma say out loud, "So you think that's funny, you son of a bitch; well, how about this." As she pulled up next to him at the red light, she rolled her window down, pulled her wig off her head, and shook it at him. I can still see that man sitting there with eyes as big as saucers and his mouth dropped open. I think Momma got the better of that exchange. Even with all of the bad things that went along with her being sick, it seems as though she always had a way to find an upside.

As all kids tend to do, we had our moments of forgetfulness about what we were supposed to be doing, but that wasn't good when it came to Momma. I had taken her back to the bathroom and helped her onto the pot with every intention of coming back in just a few minutes, but as I was going back into the living room, some of the other kids were heading outside so I joined them. After what could have only been forty minutes later, Andy told us all to shut up and listen; when all was quiet we could hear a distant cry for help. Momma was still on the toilet. She was pretty mad, not Matilda mad, but pretty mad.

CHAPTER **14**

The Summer Of '75

DURING THE SUMMER of 1975, one of the doctors from John Peter Smith recommended to Momma that she visit a group of doctors at Scott and White hospital. Supposedly they were doing some amazing things with patients with similar diseases. So on a Thursday night, we were all helping Momma and Daddy pack up clothes and medicine and all that stuff for Momma to take with her for the week. Everyone was very excited.

Aunt Linda and Uncle Dale came to get me and the five younger kids to stay with them in Mineral Wells for the week. This was like a vacation for us. They had a really nice house that had carpet, two bathrooms, and the best thing ever, air-conditioning. Aunt Linda cooked breakfast every morning; we had lunch every day and a nice supper every night. It was truly a vacation. We even went to the park and swam in a real lake. I remember thinking this must be what summer camp is like.

Again, being a kid, you never know what grown-ups talk

about. One night after I had put the girls and Jaimie to bed, I asked my aunt Linda if I could stay up a little bit longer and watch television with her and Uncle Dale. She said of course I could. After just a few minutes they turned the TV off and said they wanted to talk to me about something. Aunt Linda said that she was very impressed with the way I took care of my younger brothers and sisters and wanted me to know that my mom really appreciated all the stuff I did for her at home. My uncle then said that Momma told him that I did a lot of things that most kids would hate to do and that I never complained about anything. He told me that it takes a real man to do the stuff I do and he thanked me for taking care of his little sister. He said he knew it would be easy to bitch and complain about missing out on some stuff with the other kids, but someday I would realize that the stuff I was doing was a lot more important and I would be glad for it later. It was kind of weird, but I have always remembered that night and how it changed the way I looked at the things I did for my mom. I always knew that Momma appreciated everything, but hearing it from other grown-ups was different.

When we got back home, Momma was already back. What was thought to be a weeklong visit for her turned out to be just a waste of gas and time. Daddy said when they got there, they admitted her and started some testing right away. By the end of the second day, they told Momma and Daddy that there was nothing they could do to cure her, or even stop the progression, but they might be able to slow it down and make her more comfortable. But on the positive side, they felt as though she was over the worst part. Momma was mad that she had to spend all those hours in the car and all that money on gas to hear them tell her something she already knew.

Within a couple of days all was back to normal. Hot summer days filled with lots of kids running around in and out of the house, Momma yelling for people to shut the screen door so the flies couldn't come in. The summer was over in flash. We were all getting ready for school to start. I was going into the seventh grade and it was great. Going into junior high is a milestone in life. No more elementary school with the little kids. You got to sit closer to the back of the bus with the high school kids. The coolest thing was that you changed classes now. We had six different classes and five minutes between classes to get to our locker and get our next book and make it to class. School was great.

CHAPTER **15**

Winter Of '75

SINCE COMING BACK from Scott and White, Momma had not been admitted to the hospital for an overnight stay, so that was a good thing. She had her normal therapy sessions and stuff like that at John Peter Smith three times a week, but nothing out of the ordinary.

During her stays in the hospital, kids were not allowed in ICU and other areas of the hospital so most of us kids seldom went when Momma was there. Sometimes Daddy would take Jaimie and maybe one or two of us older kids, but for the most part we all just stayed home. In fact, I remember the last time Momma was there, Daddy took me, Trisha, and Shelly with him. He took the girls because they really wanted to see Momma and he took me so I could look after them. Daddy had told me what to do to get the girls in to see Mom. While he was talking to the lady at the counter, I was supposed to sneak the girls around the corner and into Momma's room. The plan worked perfectly. We spent about thirty minutes in Momma's room before they made us leave. Visiting hours were over. Now that I think about it, they probably knew we were sneaking in, but it was okay.

CHAPTER **16**

November '75

IT WAS NOVEMBER 12, which was a Wednesday, when Momma was admitted to the hospital this time. Again, nothing out of the ordinary; she had gone to her normal therapy session that day with Daddy. When we got home from school, he said they were going to keep her over the weekend to try some different therapy treatments on her arms and legs. My aunt Linda, Uncle Charles and their two kids came over to our house that Saturday morning just like they usually did. It was kind of cold that week, I remember. We spent most of Saturday playing football and my dad and Uncle Charles worked on my uncle's race car.

I think it was around three or four when my aunt Linda said she was going to see Momma and wanted to know who else wanted to go. We all started yelling, "Me, me, and me." Then Daddy, with his "no need to reason, because I am the dad," yelled back, "Ain't none of you going if you don't stop yelling. You know you all can't go." So my uncle Charles stepped in to save the situation.

Charles was always the fun uncle. He liked being the cool uncle who everybody wanted to hang with, so he offered this: "Why don't you boys stay here and we will all play some poker or dominoes." Of course that was all we needed to hear. So the only ones who went with Daddy and Aunt Linda were Shelly, Trisha, and Jaimie. The rest of us stayed home.

We finished cleaning up the tools and things that Daddy was using to work on the car and headed in to start playing poker while they loaded up to go to the hospital; it must have been around 5:00. It was me, Jerry, Andy, our cousin Charles Joe, and Uncle Charles playing poker. Sherrill, our cousin little Sissy and big Sissy were either playing or watching television, I don't really remember.

While we were playing cards, someone knocked on the front door. It was Howard Skinner, the grandson of our landlord. In the two or three years we lived in this house, Howard had only been there maybe twice, including tonight. He was about sixteen years old, a little strange and very shy. Anyway, when I opened the door, all he said was "Someone from John Peter Smith hospital called and wants your dad to call them." Remember, we didn't have a phone so we always gave Mr. Skinner's phone number as an emergency number to places like the schools and stuff. My uncle Charles said to us that since Daddy had only been gone thirty minutes or so and he figured he should be at the hospital any time now, he would find out what they wanted. We went back to our poker game.

We had been playing for about an hour when we stopped for dinner. Aunt Linda had put on a pot of beans and she brought bologna for sandwiches. My uncle Charles was never one to spend much time cooking, but he decided we were not going to have cold sandwiches, so he fried the bologna up and we had hot sandwiches and beans. After a quick dinner we resumed the game. I don't remember who was winning or who was losing. I just remember it was fun playing for real money without all of the grown-ups.

It must have been around 9:00 p.m. by now, and we had stopped playing poker and had teamed up to play spades. Charles Joe had gone into the living room and was asleep on the floor. Sissy and Sherrill were asleep on Momma's bed and little Sissy was asleep on the couch. We figured Daddy and the rest of them should be home any minute because *Saturday Night Wrestling* would be coming on soon and nobody wanted to miss that.

A few minutes later, we heard the car pull into the driveway. I remember hearing the car doors closing and my dad talking. A gust of cold air hit us as the front door opened. Jaimie, eight years old, was the first one in, and as he turned the corner into the kitchen, the only thing he said was "Momma died." I remember turning to look at him and just said, "You liar." But then my dad walked in right behind him carrying Shelly, who must have fallen asleep on the way home, and my dad had tears in his eyes. Then I knew. I felt the wind get sucked right out of me, because I had never seen my daddy cry, ever. Even when his parents died, he didn't cry. Aunt Linda came in behind him with Trisha. She burst into tears and starting hugging my uncle Charles. Everything I knew our family to be was turned upside down. No crying, no hugs, no "I love you," and no affection became hugging, crying, sobbing, and comforting.

NOVEMBER '75

My dad sat down in his chair, and his rugged face, which showed every year of his hard life, was soft, sad, caring, and crying. Sissy and Sherrill were still asleep on the couch, Charles Joe and little Sissy were already awake and crying. I don't think they even knew why; they were just crying because everyone else was. Sherrill was the next to wake up, and she was confused and walked over to my dad. He tried the best he could, but without much experience with this kind of thing, he just said it like it was. He told her, "Momma died today." Sissy was sitting up now on the bed and she definitely looked confused, dazed, still half asleep. Jaimie went over and said just like Daddy did, "Sissy, Momma died." Sissy took it the hardest that first night. She started screaming, "NO, NO!" My aunt Linda grabbed her and held her as she continued to cry and scream. Andy and Jerry were sitting on the couch holding Shelly and Trisha. Jamie went back to be with my dad in his chair. Sherrill went over to Linda, and she and Sissy lay in the lap and arms of Aunt Linda. Charles Joe and little Sissy were sitting one on each knee of their dad, and me, I just sat on the floor next to Momma's bed with my knees drawn up to my chest. I didn't cry. I was just sad, very, very sad. I missed her already.

Everything happened so fast. One minute we were all playing a game, and the next minute Momma was gone.

As I sat on the floor I kept thinking about the last thing Momma and I talked about that Wednesday morning. She woke me up around 4:30 that morning to get her bed pan. Afterward, I got her two pain pills and a glass of water. I think she knew that morning that her time was up. I sat on her bed next to her and she had one arm around my shoulders. She told me that soon

I wouldn't have to do all of these things for her because she was going to get better. I told her that I didn't mind doing this stuff for her. She hugged me as tight as her fragile arms could hug and said, "I love you, John Darrel, I love you so much. Now help me back to bed and you go back to sleep." She lay back as I moved her pillow under her head; then I propped two pillows under her drawn-up knees, pulled a sheet up over her, leaned over and kissed her on the forehead, and said, "I love you, too." I didn't go back to sleep. I just lay on the floor and listened for her to call me again.

That morning as we were all getting ready to go to school, we noticed that Daddy was still home; normally he was either gone or leaving when we got up. That day, he was driving Momma to her doctor's appointments, which meant that I didn't need to go. Momma was sitting up in her bed so I went over and asked her if she needed me to stay home and watch Shelly and Trisha, but she said not today. Linda was coming over to do that. I said okay and started to walk away, but then Momma stopped me and rubbed my cheek with the back of her curled fingers. She didn't say anything; she just smiled. Then all of a sudden someone heard the bus coming around the corner, and yelled, "BUS," so we all headed out the door. As usual the boys were faster and out the door first; just as the girls and Jaimie were heading out, Momma called to us, "Y'all behave."

When we got home from school that afternoon Linda told us that they had admitted Momma and she would be in the hospital for the weekend. No big deal, nothing new. The next few days were typical for us. I think Daddy went to the hospital on Thursday night with Sissy and Sherril for a couple of hours.

NOVEMBER '75

On Friday he had to work late, but my aunt Linda said that she was going up there and was going to take Granny to visit Momma, so none of us went. When Charles and Linda came over that Saturday morning, Linda said Momma was doing well and that she may get to come home on Sunday. But of course Sunday never came.

After what seemed like forever, everybody settled down. The reality had overcome the shock, and Daddy took the first step of moving on. He told us that Momma had died before they got to the hospital and they were just doing the paperwork and stuff all night. He took control of the family and blurted out the plan of action for the night. Since Jerry and Andy were the oldest, they needed to get the younger kids settled into bed. Linda volunteered to help with that since she needed to get her kids to bed as well. "John Darrel, you get Momma's wallet and all of the dimes out of the jar and come with me; we need to go into town." My aunt Linda volunteered my uncle Charles to drive us.

As we drove to the 7-Eleven in Mansfield I remember listening to my dad and uncle talk about what all needed to happen next, who needed to be called first, and how much money would be needed. I think the impact of Momma dying was not as great on my dad and the other grown-ups because they saw it coming for months and maybe years. I remember the way my brothers and sisters reacted and how it was so different than the way I reacted, as if I too had been somewhat prepared for this time by the things my mom told me and the conversations we had over the past year. I was still very sad and shocked that night, but there didn't appear to be a lingering effect. I remember sitting in the backseat of my uncle's car thinking that I would never see my mom again, and I finally started crying. My dad turned and looked at me once, but didn't say anything. He let me have my few minutes alone. The drive to town was about twenty minutes.

As we got into town my dad started telling me what he needed me to do. I pulled myself together and listened. The reason I brought dimes from the jar was to make phone calls with the pay phones at the 7-Eleven. My job was to help my dad make the phone calls. My uncle Charles was going to drive to Pawpaw and Granny's house to tell them and then come back and get Daddy and me. The first person we called was my uncle Dale. This was my mom's brother in Mineral Wells. His wife (also named Linda) answered the phone and when I said, "Aunt Linda, this is John," she immediately asked, "Is your mom okay?" I said, "No ma'am, she died tonight." Then after a couple of seconds, my uncle Dale got on the phone and all he said was "Tell your daddy we will be there in the morning." I stood there in the cold, looking through my mom's wallet, finding phone numbers of relatives and neighbors of relatives who didn't have phones. We called Daddy's boss at Trans Tex, and we called Uncle Jackie's mother-in-law. As I called uncles and friends, my dad called some of his relatives and other people I didn't know. I asked my dad if I could use one of the dimes to call Joe (my best friend) and he said I could, so I called him and told him what happened. I knew Joe would pass the word around school for me Monday. Then my uncle Charles drove up and we headed back home. Most everybody was asleep except Andy and Aunt Linda. I don't know if my dad slept at all that night, but I know I didn't. Shelly and Trisha were asleep on Momma's bed, so I just laid on the floor where I was supposed to be.

NOVEMBER '75

Sunday morning Uncle Dale, Aunt Linda, and their three girls arrived about 8:00. My uncle Melvin, Aunt Shirley, and their four girls were already there as well as my Pawpaw and Granny. The house was full of people, inside and out. I don't know how they found out so quickly, but several churches were already bringing food to our house by lunchtime.

I remember five or six of the grown-ups sitting around the table in the kitchen talking about Momma's funeral. Some of the kids were outside, some of them were in the living room with Pawpaw and Granny, and some were watching television. I was sitting quietly in the kitchen listening to the grown-ups. I learned a long time ago that if you kept quiet and did something productive, you didn't get told to go outside when the grown-ups were talking. I kept pouring coffee for everyone and emptying the ashtrays when they got full. When Uncle Dale needed a piece of paper and pencil, I was quick to say, "I got it."

My dad was not a big man by any means but he always spoke his mind and held his own. He was never really overshadowed by anyone, but that day I remember him seeming to be small. He was sitting in the chair with his chain of cigarettes and a cup of never-ending coffee, with a very sad face that looked as though he could start crying at any minute. He looked like a little boy who had lost his puppy.

I never really thought much about my mom and dad in a loving marital-type relationship, because for nearly one-third of my twelve years of living, they slept in different beds, even in different rooms in a five-room house. There were no greetings at the door with a kiss and "how was your day?" No dinners out, or date night. There never seemed to be any alone time for Momma and Daddy. That was not our family. But seeing my dad sitting in that chair discussing my mom's funeral and all that goes with it that day, I realize now that he loved her beyond what we would ever know and he was missing her already.

For a man to marry a woman who already has seven kids and take those kids in as if they were his own and then have three more kids with that woman is remarkable enough, but then to stay by her side, care for her and all of her kids for four more years when she is stricken with a disease, one that is slowly crippling her, physically takes him to a pedestal that can only be reached by a few men in this world. There may have been a little bit of lack of self-confidence in my dad, with his limited education and his poor man persona, which may have had him thinking that he had probably better stay with a woman who would have him rather than go look for a second one, but seeing him that day makes me certain that he did what he did because of his love and complete devotion to her.

As much as I assure you we never had family discussions like "how was your day at school" or "how was work today," I am just as sure that there were conversations behind closed doors, or on the trips back and forth from the hospital, or maybe while the kids were at school, but never in front of us between Momma and Daddy. Conversations about what went on or what would happen when Momma was gone; grown-up discussions about the five kids who still lived there who were the children of Herschel Conn and things like that.

As the grown-ups began talking, my uncle Dale was leading

NOVEMBER '75

the conversation. It seemed fitting, as he was probably the one who was going to put in the most money for the funeral and services. I don't remember a lot of specifics discussed that day but I remember a few things that affirm my thoughts that Momma knew it was her time to go.

Apparently, the funeral services had already been discussed and would be held at Central Baptist Church, and Pastor Rowlett would perform the services. It was told to Daddy that Saturday night when he got to the hospital, earlier that day Momma had asked to speak with a preacher. Pastor Rowlett was already at the hospital and since he was from a church in Mansfield, Momma spoke with him. What they talked about was between Momma, the preacher, and God, but Pastor Rowlett assured us that Momma had made her peace with God and they had a very open and lengthy conversation about her life, her death, and going to heaven. Having not been a very religious family, most of us couldn't really understand why Momma would ask to speak to a preacher, but I know that day when Pastor Rowlett assured us that Momma had asked God for forgiveness and that she was being welcomed into heaven with open arms, I had mixed emotions. On one hand I had a pure joy that Momma was going to heaven, but I also remember hating God for the pain and suffering that Momma had gone through for the past several years and for taking her from all of us kids who needed her so much.

A couple of the nurses who had treated my mom on that Saturday told my dad that she had a great morning. They said that Momma didn't take her pain pills that morning because she really didn't need them. They said that she ate very well and had no problem swallowing her food and that she really enjoyed her lunch. They also said that Momma sat up in the bed several times on her own and talked with them while they did their work. It had been five or six months since Momma was able to pull or push herself into a sitting position by herself. The point of all this is that it appears as though her last day alive was a good day. Very little if any pain from her feet and hands, no pain when she swallowed her food, and no pain from sitting up for extended periods of time. My granny says it was God giving her a good day for her last day. My Pawpaw says, "There is always brightness before the darkness," and my uncle Melvin says there is always calm before the storm; basically I think everybody has their own way of saying that Momma knew she was only going to be here a little while longer and that is why she asked to talk to the preacher.

I don't know if she talked with any of my brothers and sisters like she talked to me on that Wednesday morning, but I think it was her way of saying good-bye to me, without saying that she thought she was going to die, but a little something between us just in case.

The next topic was the burial place. I think Dale wanted Momma to be buried in Mineral Wells in the cemetery where other family members were buried, but Daddy said he wanted her buried here in Mansfield where she lived and where her kids lived. I don't remember Uncle Dale putting up much of an argument. So it was decided. I don't remember any discussions about the casket or anything else, but it seems like the whole meeting only took about an hour.

The only other heated conversation I remember was about what we all were going to wear to the funeral. My uncle Dale's wife, Linda, wanted to take us all to Gibson's Department Store first thing in the morning and buy all of the boys a new suit and get the girls nice dresses. She told Daddy that she would pay for everything. On one hand it made sense, everybody would look real nice and dressed up, but on the other hand I had to agree with my dad, that the money spent on those clothes would be better used buying groceries or helping pay for something else. He didn't see any use in us wearing something to Momma's funeral that we never wore before. He was fine with us wearing whatever clothes we already had.

Well, that was it. Everything was done. The funeral would be at the Blessing McInnis funeral home in Mansfield, services by Pastor Rowlett of the Central Baptist Church, with graveside services in the Mansfield Cemetery. We would wear our regular clothes and each put a picture of ourselves in the casket with Momma.

It was getting about suppertime now, so the two Aunt Lindas and my aunt Shirley ran everybody out of the kitchen so they could get supper ready.

The next morning things seemed to have slowed down. I guess most of the grown-ups went to the funeral home to finalize all of the arrangements. I think it was Daddy, Uncle Dale, and Aunt Linda. The rest of us just stayed around the house. Kids were starting to get back to doing things kids do. Some were outside playing, some were watching television, and some of us were just sitting around. Some of the adults had to go to work since it was Monday, but none of us kids went to school.

More and more people were bringing things to the house,

mainly food, but some people brought money and clothes and some even brought flowers with cards. It was strange being at home with all of Momma's stuff there. Her bed was empty, her wheelchair folded up and pushed against the wall, and her crutches were still standing in the corner next to her bed. On the table next to her bed were several bottles of lotion, some unopened boxes of gauze wrap, and several bottles of various medications. Nothing was moved as if they were just waiting for her to need them.

The day of the funeral had arrived. I don't know if it is a mental block or just time passing, but I really don't remember much of that morning, like who rode with who or what time we left for the funeral, but I do remember once we got to the funeral home.

Just inside the door there was a big book that people could sign, to show they were there and to leave any kind of message to the family. I remember standing there reading the names on the list, and recognizing people like Mrs. Carter, Joey Davis, Mr. and Mrs. Dorsey, Jack and Janice Holman, Joe Holman, and the list just went on. There were lots of flowers and some of them were huge. I remember reading some of the cards on the big ones. They were from Daddy's work, Trans Tex Supply, and one from the teachers at Erma Nash Elementary School.

We all went in the big room and sat down in the front row. I don't remember much of what Pastor Rowlett said because I was too busy looking around at all of the people. I remember trying to guess how many people were in that room. It was packed. I knew or at least recognized most of them, but there were a lot I didn't know. I was sitting next to Andy and I asked him who all these people were. He just said they were people that Momma knew, now shut up.

I can still see the coffin sitting in the front of the church surrounded by big bouquets of flowers. The coffin had something draped across it with another flower arrangement sitting on it. My granny was the first person to lose it during the funeral. She started crying really loud and calling out my momma's name. My aunt Linda got up and went over and sat next to her. She held Granny's head on her shoulder. I don't know if it was the funeral itself or Granny starting to cry, but that started the domino effect. My little sisters started to cry but I think that was because of Granny, and several other people started crying as well. I didn't start crying then; however, I started crying a few minutes later because they opened the casket.

Now was the time we were all supposed to walk by the casket and place our pictures in Momma's hand. I don't remember what order we went but I remember standing next to the casket, crying hard and not wanting to leave. I knew this was the last time I would ever see Momma. She was beautiful. She was wearing her wig but it was done up very nice. Her hands were crossed, lying on her stomach. Her face had some makeup on it but not a lot. I remember thinking that she looked different, but later I realized she looked happy or comfortable or relieved or maybe just not in pain. I didn't want to leave. I started crying harder. My aunt Linda was standing there trying to keep the line moving, but she was crying just as hard as everyone else. The last person in line was my dad. The second time in three or four days I saw Daddy crying. We all sat back down. Pawpaw called out, "Oh God, oh God." This was the first funeral I had ever been to.

I don't remember much of the service after that. I don't even remember the ride to the cemetery but I will never forget this. We were one of the first cars there and I couldn't believe how many cars came in after us. It seems like there were hundreds of cars. I am sure that has a lot to do with a twelve-year-old's exaggeration, but there were a multitude of cars. I remember thinking that my Momma had lots of friends.

It took several minutes for everyone to get from the cars to the gravesite so we all just sat in our chairs and waited. Pastor Rowlett stood at the end of the coffin and started talking and praying some more. The graveside services only lasted fifteen or twenty minutes, and then everyone started leaving. Even the family started heading to their cars. Everyone except me and my dad. My dad just sat there with his legs crossed and his hands in his lap. I moved over a chair to be next to him, and without looking up, he kept staring at the coffin and said, "Well, she won't be hurtin' no more."

Once again, I don't remember anything Pastor Rowlett said standing there in the cemetery, but as my dad got up to head to the car, I think it really hit me. Momma was right. I wouldn't have to doctor her feet and hands anymore, I wouldn't have to rub lotion on her back or legs anymore, and I wouldn't have to sleep on the floor next to her bed ever again. She was all better.

On the ride home I don't remember anyone talking. Not even the girls. No fighting, no crying, nothing. I sat next to the window and just stared out. I thought about all the times I stayed home from school with my mom. How we used to watch television together when the little ones were napping. Our favorite show was *Perry Mason*. Momma always wanted me to be a lawyer. When we needed to go somewhere, sometimes she would move the seat all the way back so I could sit on the seat in front of her and drive the car while she worked the pedals. Of course I could never say anything to the other kids.

As we got closer to the house, I knew that everything had changed. Our lives were never going to be the same. I heard Daddy talking to my aunt Linda in the front seat. I couldn't hear everything but I knew something was up. Daddy didn't know how to take care of all these kids. He couldn't stay home with them during the day.

When we got home, everybody else was already there, all of Momma's brothers and sisters, with all of their kids, and Pawpaw and Granny. There were lots of people I didn't know. Pastor Rowlett was there and even the preacher from the Baptist church in Webb. Mrs. Parker and Mrs. Holman were leaving; they had just come by to drop off some food. There was so much food. I can honestly say that I had never seen so much in one place. It seemed like hours had gone by before everybody left. I figure it was around six or so because it was starting to get dark. I remember it was getting dark because just after everyone was gone, a car pulled up in the driveway. We saw the lights flash across the living room wall, and I figured someone forgot something and was just coming back to get it. I got up and was standing at the front door waiting for them to come in. After a couple of minutes it hit me. I knew this person, I recognized him, and more importantly I recognized the other man with him. It was Rocky and Herschel. We all ran to Rocky. What a surprise! We hadn't seen him for several years. Not since that day he and Daddy had the fight in the backyard. He looked all grown up. They came from Georgia for Momma's funeral but were late getting there from the airport, so they missed it.

After everyone settled down, several of the grown-ups went to the kitchen and were sitting around the table. After just a few minutes my dad called me, Andy, Jerry, Sissy, and Sherrill into the kitchen. When we walked in, I remember him sitting there just looking at the floor, cross-legged with a cup of coffee in one hand and a cigarette in the other. As we all made our way into the kitchen, he looked up at us and in what may be the second hardest thing he had had to face in his life, coming just three days after the hardest, he said with a trembling soft voice, and I remember it verbatim, "Y'alls real daddy wants to take all of you with him; he says he has a big house in Georgia and says all of you can come live with him. I can't give you what he can, I can't give you much more than a roof over your head and some food in your belly, but every damn one of you is welcome to stay here with us as long as you want and I think that is what your momma would want, but it's your choice." I was the first to move. I walked over to my dad and put my hand on his shoulder and said, "I ain't going anywhere." I think Sissy and Sherrill weren't quite sure what was going on, but they followed behind me; Sissy stood behind me and Sherrill climbed into Daddy's lap. Jerry was next, and said something like, "I'm staying home," and then Andy commented that he only had a year left in high school so he wasn't going anywhere either. As best as I can recall, that was it. Herschel stood up and told Rocky to come on, it was time to go. As they walked out the door, none of us moved. We all stood right there beside Daddy, nobody knowing what to say

NOVEMBER '75

or do, but then my uncle Charles yelled out, "Hell yeah, let's eat some of those pies." That was it. Situation over.

That night was very strange. It was as if things were supposed to go back to a normal life, but there was no Momma. The last couple of days were filled with people coming and going, no school, the funeral, Herschel showing up out of nowhere. Lots of things happening, but that night was the first night with nobody there but our family. Well, almost nobody. Sometime during that evening, it was decided that Charles and Linda, with their two kids, would move in with us to help take care of the little ones. It would only be another year before Shelly would be in kindergarten, so it made sense.

Daddy would move out of the added-on bedroom and Charles and Linda would have it. Daddy would take one of the bunk beds in the bedroom with all of the kids. Simple enough.

I was sitting on the floor leaning against Momma's bed, several kids were lying on the floor, Charles and Linda were sitting on the couch, and Daddy was in his chair with Shelly and Trisha sitting on his lap. I looked around and realized that everything was almost normal. Here we were, Saturday night westerns and variety shows on TV, all the kids lying around, Momma's bed was still in the living room. Nothing was moved: all of her medicine was still sitting on the table, her crutches were still leaning against the wall at the head of the bed, her bed pan was still sitting under the bed, her water glass was still sitting on the table half full of water, there was an empty Dr. Pepper bottle sitting next to it, and her wheelchair was right where it had been for the last year or so. The only thing different: no Momma.

I was one of the last ones to go to bed that night. It was just after *Saturday Night Wrestling*. Daddy was still sitting in his chair, but Shelly and Trisha were in bed. Charles was sitting on the couch, and Linda was lying on the couch with her head on Charles' lap. Andy was still lying on the floor next to the heater. I looked over at Daddy and as he turned to look at me, I asked him if I could sleep in Momma's bed that night. He didn't say anything; he just nodded and turned away. I knew we were going to have to move her bed soon, so I thought it would be my last chance to be next to it.

The next morning we were all up pretty early. When I got up, everybody was doing normal stuff. Daddy and Charles were outside working on Andy's car. Linda was in the kitchen cleaning and organizing all of the food. There were a couple of kids watching TV and several were outside. I know there were a couple still asleep but I don't know who. Anyway, I went into the kitchen and sat at the table. Linda turned from the sink and said, "Good morning, sleepy head." I didn't say anything. I just started nibbling on the food sitting on the table. Coming from a woman I have personally seen in a fistfight with my mom, a woman with tattoos on several parts of her body, a woman I know could beat up most men, what she said to me that morning really blew me away. She didn't come over and hug me or hold me or anything like that; she just looked at me over her shoulder from the sink while she was doing dishes and said, "You know your momma is in heaven and she is going to be so proud of the man you are going to be someday. She always told me how much you took care of her. You're a good boy and she loved you very much." I ate a little bit more and thought about what she said. After a few minutes I went outside and starting helping my dad and uncle.

NOVEMBER '75

Later that afternoon, Daddy and Charles left for a bit and came back with another couch. We replaced Momma's bed with the couch. Daddy let me put all of her medicine, bandages, gauze wrap, and lotions into a small box. I put it in the closet in our bedroom with her crutches. Daddy said he was going to give the bed to our uncle Melvin, since they needed it. We rearranged the living room after taking all of Momma's stuff out, and just like that, everything was done. We were officially moving on.

I honestly don't remember much about anything for a while after that weekend. I know Christmas was hard. Momma's birthday was December 19, and even though we never celebrated anyone's birthday, that year was different. Daddy took us all out to Momma's grave on her birthday. We didn't really know what to do, so we all just stood around and looked at the ground. Then Jerry said something funny that Momma had done one time when she couldn't get her fingers to work the way she wanted, and of course then we all started telling our favorite funny thing that Momma said or did. We must have stayed there for an hour and then the laughter died down. Daddy told us all to say good-bye and start heading to the truck.

The thing I remember most about that visit was that Momma didn't have a headstone. She just had a marker stuck in the ground with her name and birthdate and the day she died on it. When we got home, I asked my aunt Linda why we didn't have a big stone marker like all of the other graves. She explained to me that they cost a lot of money and with all of the funeral cost and the money the hospital wanted, there just wasn't enough to buy a headstone, but they had planned on saving up to get one.

As the winter turned to spring and spring to summer, all of a sudden it had been a year since Momma died. Then before you turned around, it had been two years. Andy was out of high school, Jerry dropped out of school, and I was in high school. The little kids were not so little anymore and time marched on.

I always thought about Momma not having a headstone and that kind of bothered me. I decided I was going to get her one. That spring I got a job at the cotton gin in Webb. I was only fourteen years old, so I couldn't run any of the machinery, but I could pack cotton seeds as they came out of the gin into the baskets, so that is what I did. I worked about twenty hours a week for $1.75 an hour. I usually gave Daddy half of my check to help pay bills at home, but the other half was going to get Momma a headstone. When the fall came around, I would get off the bus at the cotton gin after school and work a few hours every other day or so. I did this for about a year, saving as much as $15 a week. It was a lot of money to me, but not enough to buy a headstone. I needed to make more money and needed to work more hours. When I was fifteen, I got a job at Lee's Supermarket in Mansfield. Daddy bought me my first car. It was a 1965 Chevy pickup. It barely ran, the floorboard was rusted out, it was beat to hell, no heat or air-conditioning, but it only cost $150 and it did the job. It allowed me to get a real job. As a sacker at Lee's I could work after school and on weekends and more importantly I made $3.25 an hour. It only took me six months to save up enough money to get the headstone for Momma's grave. I didn't ask anyone to help, I didn't tell anyone I was doing it. I just handled it myself. It took several days after I ordered it for them to make it and deliver it to her grave, but I remember

NOVEMBER '75

going out there the first time to see it and how proud I was. She deserved a nice marker telling the world that she was the best mom.

Moms are the best, there is no doubt. Looking at my life for the first fifteen or so years, I felt as though we were cheated by not having a mom like all of the other kids. But now as an adult, I look back and think maybe I was very lucky, in the fact that I had three moms. Barbara Parker, Janice Holman, and of course my mom.

While I am not wealthy, famous, or anything like that, I do consider myself very fortunate for the way my life turned out. In the grand scheme of things, I have turned out very successfully despite my background, and I owe it all to the people who influenced my life during the time of my mom's sickness, her passing, and the several years to follow.

Mr. Howard the bus driver made sure I was thinking of others, he always had a kind word for me, and he made sure I looked at things in a positive manner. The first thing he asked me every morning was "How is your momma today?"

Barbara Parker was my mom at school. I have never known a kinder person. I am quite certain that she did for many other kids in school the things she did for me, but I don't know if any of them learned what I learned from her. Just from her actions, I know that I have more compassion, I am more generous and care more for other people. She showed me that giving to others, even at the expense or sacrifice of yourself, is okay. She never looked for thanks or recognition or praise; she just did what she knew needed to be done at that moment. She is and always has been an amazing person and I loved her like my very own mom.

Janice Holman was my other at-home mom. I spent so much time at Joe's house during my teenage years that Janice was truly my mom. She was never quite the tender-hearted, giving mom that Barbara was, but I am here today to tell you that without her no-nonsense, hard-handed, and straightforward love, I would have probably ended up like several of my brothers, who dropped out of high school, went to jail on several occasions, and never lived up to their potential. Janice, who told me to call her Mom from the time I was ten, had three other sons and knew how to handle boys. She was tough, fair, and determined to make sure I succeeded in life.

For many years I was angry at God for putting my mom through the four years of being sick, suffering with physical pain on a daily basis, allowing her to suffer the emotional pain she endured, making her struggle both physically and mentally with her babies, and then taking her from so many kids who needed a mom and putting our family through such hard times. But I see how my life turned out and maybe, just maybe, I am the way I am today because of all of the influences of the people who were introduced into my life because of my mom's situation, and for that I am very thankful.

Forty years later I still miss my mom and am sure I always will. I think of her every day. My amazing wife of thirty-two years reminds me that I am truly a lucky man. As my two boys have grown to be amazing young men, I think back to what my life could have been and I am grateful for all of the events and people that shaped me into the man I am. Momma never complained, never made excuses, and never felt sorry for herself. She played the hand she was dealt and did the best she could with it. She was the strongest person I have ever known. I know she always wanted more for her kids than what she had; she wanted us to break the cycle our family was in, and I owe it to several people, but I think I have done that. Like my aunt Linda said the day after the funeral, I think my mom would be proud of the man I have become. I know she is all better and I think because of her, I am too.

CPSIA information can be obtained
at www.ICGtesting.com
Printed in the USA
LVHW112317010822
724938LV00004B/55